ANDREW JOHNSON

ANDREW JOHNSON

by

Edwin P. Hoyt

REILLY & LEE CO.

Chicago • 1965

TABLE OF CONTENTS

✪

1 | ☆

President By Chance

On the first day of March, 1865, Andrew Johnson arrived in Washington, D. C., and went to the Kirkwood House, a hotel on the corner of Pennsylvania Avenue and Tenth Street, where, a hundred years later, the Hotel Raleigh would stand. He had come from Tennessee to be inaugurated Vice-President of the United States of America under President Abraham Lincoln.

Johnson seemed a strange choice for the Vice-Presidency, perhaps, but these were strange times. He was a crude man in many ways. He had not learned to write until he was nineteen years old, and he had been taught that useful art by his wife. By trade he was a tailor. By nature he was a backwoods statesman and politician, fiercely loyal to the Union and to the concept of Popular Democracy that had grown up in the days of Andrew Jackson. To Andy Johnson, Tennessee tailor, congressman, governor, and senator, the people were supreme; theirs was the only authority he recognized. He had little use for the highly-educated men who flocked to official Washington during the war and paraded their wealth and superiority before the people. He had said so many times, and he was to say so again. He was a man of the people, a heavy-faced, long-nosed man with high forehead and hair that would have seemed graceful on another, but was unimpressive on his craggy features. His eyes were deepset. His brow was wrinkled with care, and his mouth turned down at the corners; deep lines lay parallel to mouth and nose along his cheeks. Even from the corners of his eyes came lines to parallel those of the rest of the face. His face was blotched—he appeared to be a heavy drinker. Indeed, the capital was alive with stories about Vice-President Johnson's drinking. But, of course, few of those around him knew that he suffered even then from the circulatory system disease that would kill him ten years later.

The man who had been elected Vice-President was chosen by Lincoln to run with him in 1864, because he was a loyal citizen from the state of Tennessee, which was a part of the South, although citizens were divided in their loyalties and the state was out of the Confederacy; and because before the war Johnson had been a Democrat. Now he, along with Abraham Lincoln, had pledged himself to loyalty to the Union party.

The Union party existed more as myth than as reality during Andrew Johnson's period in office, but during the summer and fall of 1864, it was a reality. There was a putting aside of narrow political views by those who supported the Union's cause in the war.

In this March of 1865, when Andrew Johnson arrived in Washington, the national capital was waiting to hear of the collapse of the Confederacy. The war was all but over. Sherman had marched into Atlanta and on to the sea, and Petersburg, Virginia, was under heavy fire. Nowhere did it seem possible that the Confederate forces would be able to win, or even survive.

On March 4, the new administration was brought into office. Lincoln took his oath of office and delivered his brief inaugural address on the south front of the Capitol, pledging to bind up the nation's wounds—to heal the wounds and scars of four years of civil war. Lincoln knew how he intended to go about this task, too.

He had no intention of permitting the politicians of the North to destroy the economy of the South. He had no thought of allowing even his own Republican party to take control of southern politics. He had proclaimed the freedom of the slaves, but he had no hatred of the South or of southerners. He envisaged an orderly program of reconstruction under which the South would be brought back into the federal government—the Senate and the House of Representatives—just as soon as the loyalties of the states could be assured. Lincoln did not talk about punishment, or about bringing into effect a social revolution. Here he was quite at odds with the radical Republicans of his party, who believed that the South should be punished, forced to bear the major cost of the war as far as possible, and that the freedom of the Negro could be assured only by a social revoluion in which the control of the economy of the South would be taken out of old hands and put into new ones.

On that same March 4, Andrew Johnson took the oath of office as Vice-President from the Chief Justice of the United States Supreme Court, Salmon P. Chase of Ohio. The ceremony took place in the Senate Chamber.

That morning, on the way to the Capitol, Andrew Johnson had complained to retiring Vice-President Hannibal Hamlin of a fever and illness for which, he said, his physician had prescribed whisky. That was not unusual; doctors often prescribed whisky for ailments in those days. But it was unusual that the incoming Vice-President would be so unwise as to drink any quantity of liquor on the way to take the oath of office and make his inaugural speech in the Senate Chamber in which he would afterward preside. Hannibal Hamlin found a flask of brandy on the way to the Capitol that day, and Andrew Johnson drank most of it before they arrived.

After the inauguration, it was the custom for the Vice-President to deliver an address in the Senate. Usually these addresses were as formal, if not as important, as those of the chief executives. But when Andrew Johnson rose to speak, he seemed red-faced and slightly unkempt. His hair was not in place; his eyes were watery. Those near him could smell liquor on his breath.

At best, Andrew Johnson was not a gentleman of the ruffed lace and starched linen school. He had no formal education, and with a kind of defiant pride he always let that be known. In Tennessee, where few men of the backwoods were educated, there was no shame or belittlement attached to a self-made man. But this was Washington, home of diplomats and the parade ground of the very wealthy of the land. It was expected that the speech of the Vice-President would be a dignified call to duty. Instead, Johnson stood up without a manuscript in his hand, a fact that was noticed immediately with whispers by many in the chamber. He began to speak. He spoke thickly, the alcohol having done its work, and he spoke to the point that he was a humble man, a man sent to Washington by the people. He turned to the cabinet officers near him and reminded them that they, too, owed all to the common people. He could not have struck a worse note, for these men, most of whom were enemies of Lincoln and his homespun ways saw no need to accept such chiding from the Vice-President. Andrew Johnson's plain, heavy talk was greeted by sneers.

This was his introduction to high national office. It was prophetic, in a way, for except for a very brief period, Andrew Johnson would be misrepresented, insulted, and reviled during the almost complete Presidential term that he was to serve as the nation's highest executive.

After the inauguration, Vice-President Johnson went out to Silver Spring, Maryland, to stay with a friend for a few days. The Congress ended its sessions just before the inauguration of the new administration. Under normal conditions there would have been no sessions of the Senate for several months—not until the following winter. Eighteen sixty-five, however, was not a normal year; it was a war year, and a special session of Congress was called. But Andrew Johnson did not preside over it. He was ill with the same fever that had driven him to drink liquor before his inauguration, a fever which kept him shivering in bed, red-faced and perspiring.

During the special session of Congress there was much talk on the floor of the Senate about Andrew Johnson. He was not unknown there, having been a senator. He had friends and enemies, and among the latter there was discussion about asking him to resign. Further, an indirect insult was offered to him when some of these enemies brought up a resolution prohibiting liquor in the Capitol restaurants.

Johnson recovered from his fever, and as he did so his face cleared, his brow became less furrowed, and he returned to Washington to take part in the political life of the capital in the last days of the war.

Although Abraham Lincoln talked of conciliation, Andrew Johnson followed a harsher line—one that appealed to the radicals of the Senate. He spoke of "hanging traitors," and the radical senators began to believe they might have misjudged the Vice-President. Specifically, Johnson talked about hanging Jefferson Davis and the other leaders of the Confederacy. Thaddeus Stevens and Senator Ben Wade heard these words and nodded sagely. They were said in the heat of the moment, and did not represent the position of the administration, or even the clear thought of the Vice-President. But the statements were made, and they created an impression in the United States Senate.

On April 2, 1865, a Sunday, the Confederate government fled from Richmond, and it was apparent that the war could last but a few days longer. A week later came the surrender of General Robert E. Lee at Appomattox Court House. On that day Andrew Johnson joined President Lincoln and others on a brief visit to Richmond, a symbolic visit, showing that once again what had been the capital of a separate nation was a part of the United States of America.

Five days later, on Good Friday, Vice-President Johnson spent some time in the evening talking with Leonard Farwell, former governor of Wisconsin. Then Farwell said that he was going to drop in at Ford's Theater, about two blocks from the Kirkwood House, to see a performance of Laura Keane in the drama *Our American Cousin*. The President and Mrs. Lincoln were attending the theater that night, too.

Vice-President Johnson went to bed quite early, after Farwell's departure. He was nearly asleep when he heard a pounding and shouting outside his room. As he arose, he could make out the voice on the other side of the door.

"Vice-President Johnson" came the shout, "if you are in this room, I must see you." He opened the door and saw his friend Farwell trying to peer over the transom. Quickly he let the former governor into the room, and was told that someone had shot the President.

At first Andrew Johnson thought he must be the victim of a joke. Then he saw Farwell's face, and he believed. The two men remained together in the room, not knowing what was to happen next. Farwell opened the door for a moment, looked up and down the hall, and shouted for servants to come and bring guards to assure the safety of the Vice-President—to admit no one to the room.

A knock sounded on the door, but Farwell would not open it until he recognized the voice of a congressman he knew. The congressman told Farwell and the Vice-President that there were five hundred people milling about worriedly in the lobby of the hotel. Andrew Johnson realized, then, that if anything was to be done in this hour of crisis, he must take the lead. He must go to President Lincoln and discover for himself what had happened.

The Vice-President was dressing in the bedroom of the two-room suite while Farwell and the congressman talked. He came out, poking his shirttail into his trousers, and told Farwell to go back to the theater and find out how the President was.

The former governor went away, and returned a short time later with the provost marshal of the District of Columbia. Farwell said that the President was dying, that Secretary of State Seward was dead, and that there was a plot afoot to kill the Vice-President and all the cabinet members.

It would have been easy enough to believe that this was so. Washington had seethed with espionage and treason and threats of assassination for four long years. Feeling ran high in some parts of the South against the Union victory. The war was scarcely ended; peace had come not a week before. It was possible to believe anything.

The provost marshal—for Washington was still a martial city—said he thought the Vice-President ought to remain exactly where he was, inside the hotel in the safe company of his friends. Johnson refused. His place was with the President, he said. But that moment was no time for argument. The Vice-President's friends were determined to protect him.

As the group in the Kirkwood House discussed the next

move, at the house near the Ford Theater where Lincoln
had been carried, Secretary of War Stanton had taken
charge. He already knew that John Wilkes Booth had shot
President Lincoln in the head. He wrote a short note to
Chief Justice Chase, telling him to be ready to administer
the oath of office to Vice-President Johnson, because Lincoln
was dying. He also sent word to the Vice-President, and a
special guard to protect Johnson.

The guard was a man named John Lee. He went to the
Kirkwood House, called on the Vice-President, and then
began to look over the building. He went to the roof, then
into the bar, where he was told by a customer that a sus-
picious-looking fellow who had been asking questions about
Vice-President Johnson had taken a room at the hotel the
day before. Detective Lee went to the hotel register, and discovered that the only name unknown to the assistant manager was that of G. Atzerodt. Atzerodt's room was silent
when he knocked. He received permission and broke down
the door. Inside he discovered a pistol, a bankbook made
out to J. Wilkes Booth, some cartridges, personal effects, a
large bowie knife, and a map of Virginia. It was apparent
that there was a conspiracy to do away with the Vice-President as well as with President Lincoln.

After Johnson received the message from Stanton, he
insisted on going to the Peterson house where Lincoln lay.
He refused a carriage or a guard of soldiers and insisted on
walking. So walk he did, accompanied by Farwell and the
provost marshal. It was a strange, silent walk, with the Vice-
President striding along, his hat down over his eyes and his
hands jammed inside his overcoat pockets.

At the Peterson house, they saw two soldiers patrolling
outside, and a little knot of civilians. It was quiet in the
very early hours of the morning. The Vice-President went
inside, into the bedroom where Lincoln lay unconscious.

Then he stopped to take Robert Lincoln's hand and murmur a few words to the son of the dying President. He left
the room somberly and walked into the front room where
Mrs. Lincoln stood. There he took her hand for a moment
and then stepped out of the house and down the street,
making his way back to the Kirkwood House to wait.

He waited through what remained of the night and into
the morning. Just after 7:22 on the morning of April 15,
Abraham Lincoln died. A letter drawn much earlier by the
order of Secretary Stanton was dispatched to Kirkwood
House. It said:

Sir:

Abraham Lincoln, President of the United States,
was shot by an assassin last evening at Ford's theater, in this
city and died at the hour of ————.

About the same time at which the President was shot, an
assassin entered the sick chamber of the Hon. William H.
Seward, Secretary of State, and stabbed him in several places
—in the throat, neck, and face—severely, if not mortally,
wounding him. Other members of the Secretary's family
were dangerously wounded by the assassin while making his
escape.

By the death of President Lincoln the office of President
has devolved under the Constitution upon you. The emergency of the government demands that you should immediately qualify according to the requirements of the
Constitution, and enter upon the duties of President of the
United States. If you will please make known your pleasure
such arrangements as you deem proper will be made.

Your obedient servants,
Hugh McCulloch, Secretary of the Treasury

Edwin M. Stanton, Secretary of War
Gideon Welles, Secretary of the Navy
W. Dennison, Postmaster General
J. P. Usher, Secretary of the Interior
James Speed, Attorney General

to Hon. Andrew Johnson,
Vice-President of the United States.

The letter was delivered by Attorney General Speed and Secretary McCulloch that morning, and around eleven o'clock the oath of office was administered to Andrew Johnson at the Kirkwood House. Chief Justice Chase pronounced the solemn words. Andrew Johnson kissed the Bible at the twenty-first verse of the eleventh chapter of Ezekiel. He was the Seventeenth President of the United States.

"You are President," said Chief Justice Chase, extending his hand in congratulation. "May God support, guide, and bless you in your administration."

President Johnson spoke a few quiet words to the handful of high officials who stood in the room. There was nothing reminiscent of that terrible day at the Capitol, when he had been ill with fever, and had made so negative an impression on the crowd of politicians and diplomats who had come to witness the event. Johnson's words on the day that he became President were thoughtful and sad. He was nearly overwhelmed by the assassination, he said. He would have to develop his policy as President slowly, as he went along. He asked for the help of all present. He offered no assurance but his own promise of hard work.

The new President's manner was impressive to the men around him. They liked what they saw, and that liking was evident in the newspaper reports of the quiet scene.

On that same day, April 15, 1865, President Johnson held his first cabinet meeting in the office of the Secretary of the Treasury. He informed the cabinet members that he would pursue the policies followed by Lincoln, and asked them all to remain in office. Usher, the Secretary of Interior, had indicated his own desire to resign, so President Johnson offered the job to James Harlan.

In the discussion that day, as later, the cabinet officers were well impressed with the attitude of the new chief executive. He seemed composed and sure of what he was doing. There was no confusion or hesitation once the enormity of his responsibility was understood.

He was generally praised for the evenness of his behaviour, from his conduct of cabinet affairs to the gentleness with which he treated the grieving widow of Abraham Lincoln. President Johnson took offices in the Treasury Building, next to the Secretary of the Treasury, and remained there for more than a month, giving Mrs. Lincoln and the family time to make plans and move.

Truly, while the Confederacy was defeated by the time that Abraham Lincoln was assassinated, the war was not yet over. The last Confederate general, E. Kirby Smith did not surrender until May 26, the day after Andrew Johnson occupied the White House. Then, on the heels of a great Union parade in Washington, the armies were disbanded, and the city which had been dominated by soldiers in uniform was once again dominated by political leaders.

The year 1865 was a new beginning for the Union. Around Washington swarmed various pressure groups and alignments. Foremost among these were the radicals, who represented the beliefs of the old abolitionists, besides those of other elements—some of them noble and some of them not. There were men like Congressman James A. Garfield of Ohio who firmly believed that the South must be pun-

ished for the toll of blood and financial disaster it had
wreaked upon the Union. There were carpetbaggers (although the term was not then as well known as it was to be
later), who derived their name from the cheap bags in
which they could carry all their possessions as they moved
from the North into the South to take government power
and jam their pockets with stolen money.

There were also War Democrats, men of the party to
which Johnson had belonged, men who had been honest
supporters of the Union during the Civil War. To Washington now came men who had not visited the city for four
long years—southerners who came to plead for rapid restoration of their former rights. There had to be some orderly
manner in which to restore the states of the South to the
Union and bring them into the national government once
again.

Obviously, the men who had fought against the southerners were wary of allowing those same enemies to sit in
the high councils of the government. This was the basic
problem. It was complicated by the firm belief of the radicals that the economic structure of the South was drifting
right back to its prewar condition. They believed that unless
drastic action was taken, slavery would not be dead at all,
but would only have changed its name. Their answer was
harsh: it was to declare all who had fought against the Union
to be enemies, to seize their property, to break up the big
estates, and to grant the Negroes full citizenship and bring
them into the government immediately.

As with any chief executive who succeeded to power overnight, President Johnson needed time to develop policies
of government. He declined to commit himself to any line.
The White House was open to all points of view; the President would see anyone but original secessionists and known
Copperheads—men in the North who sympathized with the

secessionists during the war years. He did declare himself
again and again as favoring punishment of conscious traitors. By these he meant the leaders of the Confederacy, including Jefferson Davis.

Within a month after he took office, the first indications
of the direction of his policy were given in an amnesty proc-
lamation. The President granted pardon to southerners,
and restoration of their property (except slaves), if they
would take an oath of allegiance to the Constitution and
agree to support the emancipation laws. Some southerners
were excluded from this amnesty: men who had left offices
in the U.S. government to join the Confederacy, rebel officers above the rank of colonel, and those whose property
was valued at more than $20,000. This last provision showed
that Johnson was aware of the sources of the rebellion. He
told a visiting delegation from Virginia that the property
clause had been placed in the amnesty because "it was the
wealthy men of the South who dragooned the people into
secession."

As time went on, and President Johnson continued to see
southerners and hear their stories, he became convinced
that the South was truly repentant, and had realized the
truth uttered years before by authors and others: Slavery
was not only wrong, it was economically unsound.

The President heard stories of the poverty of the southerners, and his heart was softened. He knew that the South's
railroads were destroyed, and banks were closed, and her
industries, such as they were, were worn out. He still believed that Jefferson Davis and other leaders should be
punished with death, but he put an end to the mistreatment
of Davis, who was kept in irons.

In the beginning, General Robert E. Lee was included
with Jefferson Davis as one who ought to be punished, but
it became apparent to all northern leaders that the common

people of the North and the South would not stand for such treatment. Lee was the hero of both sides; he commanded the loyalty of southerners and the respect of all his enemies. A few months after the surrender at Appomattox, General Lee became president of Washington and Lee University, and from that position used his influence to convince southerners that Andrew Johnson and his administration were doing the best they could do to "bind up the nation's wounds," as Lincoln had asked.

Johnson came into office an unpopular man, but quickly gained the respect of Washington officialdom and the public outside. He was speedy in pressing the trial and punishment of the conspirators who had assassinated President Lincoln. He was so outspoken about the need for punishing southern leaders that Senator Ben Wade, one of the leading radicals, advised the President against executing more than a dozen of the rebels—the Senator feared that the President might go too far if unchecked. Even before the state funeral of Lincoln was complete, the radicals of Congress held a caucus and agreed among themselves that President Johnson was doing just what they wanted. That was the day on which Senator Ben Wade made the statement:

"Johnson," he said, "by the gods we have faith in you; there will be no further trouble with rebels now."

Southerners began to praise Johnson, although a few years before they had damned him as a traitor to the people of his own state for sticking with the Union. War Democrats of the North supported him, and so did the old Whig leaders who had struggled to maintain the Union for many years.

By the end of the first eight months of his term—in December, 1865—President Andrew Johnson seemed to have the nation solidly behind him. Three-fourths of the states had ratified the Thirteenth Amendment to the Constitution, and slavery was abolished by constitutional law. Congress met on December 6, and nearly every southern state was represented there. The southerners had called conventions, pledged their renewed loyalty to the Union, chosen congressmen and senators, and had restored civil government within the Union to the South.

President Johnson's first state paper, his message to Congress, was greeted with pleased amazement at home and abroad. He had been depicted for so long as a brutal lout that many, particularly in the South, could not believe that he could issue so eloquent and dignified an address. He said that the term "state sovereignty" was a Confederate term, not representative of the language of the Constitution of the United States. He said that the Constitution of the United States was the supreme law of the land and that its authority guaranteed the security of the states. He called for patience in the trials ahead as the two races began to live side by side, hoping for "mutual benefit and good will." He spoke out against monopolies and class legislation. He praised the South for having retaken its place in the Union.

So by the end of this first eight months, with Lincoln's assassins punished, and many Confederate leaders and officers in jail, and with the southern states coming back into Congress, it appeared that a relatively painless binding up of the wounds of the nation was taking place. The writ of *habaeas corpus* was still suspended in the South, which meant that men could be arrested and held without charge. Troops were still stationed in some areas of the South to preserve order. Yet, few of those troops wished to remain; the sentiment was overwhelmingly in favor of peaceful transition.

Unnoticed, however, little clouds had begun to rise on the horizon. The Mississippi state legislature had raised an insistent cry that Jefferson Davis must be pardoned by Presi-

dent Johnson (although Davis steadfastly refused to ask for
pardon because he said he had done nothing wrong). The
temporary governor of the state of South Carolina had expressed sorrow at having to bring his state back into the
Union. In the North, Copperhead sympathizers began to
praise Johnson. And all this, coupled with the praise from
the South, brought about some uneasiness among the political leaders of the Union forces in Congress.

So at the same time that President Johnson was receiving
national praise, the radical leaders of Congress were meeting
in Washington, determined to put an end to a threat they
saw to Republican power. Almost overnight they were to
swing Congress and then the country against the President.
It was to be one of the most complete and far-reaching turn-
abouts in American history. The result was to be the aban-
donment of Abraham Lincoln's hopes for orderly reconstruction of the damage caused by war, and the changeover
to a policy of harsh punishment of the South. Much of the
reason for the failure of Lincoln's policy (which was also
Johnson's) lies in the nature of Andrew Johnson, in his re-
lationship to the war effort and national effort of the past,
and in the struggle between this man, the Chief Executive,
and a Congress that insisted on keeping power. As far as
the story of this period can be that of any one man, it is the
story of Andrew Johnson, Seventeenth President of the
United States.

2 | ☆

The Boy From the Smokies

Among the most important influences in the shaping of the character of Andrew Johnson were the circumstances of his birth and early years. Andrew Johnson was born on December 29, 1808, in a little cottage in the yard of Casso's Inn in Raleigh, North Carolina. His father and mother were among the class of poor whites of the South. "Plebeians," they were called. They themselves recognized the lowliness of their station.

In the South of the early Nineteenth Century, there was no middle class. Either a man had property, including slaves, or he had no property. If he had nothing, he was a poor white; if he did manual labor, he had no status in the community.

Jacob Johnson, Andrew's father, was an honest man, and if he was little respected by the influential people of Raleigh in his life, he at least earned their respect in his death. One day in the winter of 1811, when a party of men had gathered at Hunter's Mill for drinking and general companionability, two of the gentlemen set out in a canoe for midstream. They were in ten feet of water when one of the men rocked the canoe, and it overturned. Jacob Johnson leaped into the stream and saved the two men. But he fell ill and died of pneumonia.

One of the men he had rescued was Colonel Tom Henderson, owner of the Raleigh *Star*, who wrote a eulogy of Jacob
Johnson in his newspaper. So while little Andrew Johnson
came into the world as a member of the lower class, he was
at least distinguished as the son of a hero. The family was
without money. Andrew's elder brother, William, was eight
years old, and Andrew was three when Jacob Johnson died.
Andrew's mother, Polly, had nowhere to turn except to her
own wits for survival. She found or begged a hand loom
somewhere and went into business spinning thread and
weaving cloth.

Polly Johnson could not support her family, no matter
how hard she worked. Two years later, William was apprenticed to Editor Henderson, and later to J. J. Selby, a tailor
in the town. When Andrew was fourteen years old, he too
was apprenticed to the tailor, to be bound until he was
twenty-one.

Actually, such apprenticeship was very nearly a form of
slavery. He was *bound*, which meant that until he was
twenty-one years old he could do nothing that his employer
did not want him to do.

That is where the trouble began. Andrew learned very
little from books. He was taught his ABC's by a friendly
educated man in the community, but there was little time
for book learning. The foreman of the tailor shop, a man
named Litchford, also tried to teach Andrew but the lessons
were given as the boy worked his needle.

Andrew was not a good apprentice. He was stubborn and
willful. He ran off into the woods to swim or hunt whenever
he felt that he could escape safely. After two years, he ran
away from his master. There are several stories which give
reasons for his escape. One has it that his master insulted
him, and Andrew struck back with his fist. Another story
says that Andrew and three other boys threw rocks at an

old woman's house one night, and the old woman threatened to have them arrested the next day.

At any rate, Andrew fled. Tailor Selby put an advertisement in the Raleigh *Gazette,* on June 24, 1824, which told the story:

TEN DOLLARS REWARD

Ran away from the Subscriber, on the night of the 15th instant, two apprentice boys, legally bound, named *William* and *Andrew* Johnson. The former is of a dark complexion, black hair, eyes, and habits. They are much of a height, about 5 feet 4 or 5 inches. The latter is very fleshy, with freckled face, light hair, and fair complexion. They went off with two other apprentices, advertised by Messrs. Wm. & Charles Fowler. When they went away, they were well clad—blue cloth coats, light colored homespun coats, and new hats, the maker's name in the crown of the hats is Theodore Clark. I will pay the above Reward to any person who will deliver said apprentices to me in Raleigh, or I will give the above Reward for Andrew Johnson alone.

All persons are cautioned against harboring or employing said apprentices on pain of being prosecuted.

James J. Selby, Tailor

Raleigh, N. C., June 24, 1824

Mr. Selby must have been agitated when he put the advertisement in the newspaper. He mixed up the descriptions of Andrew and his brother, for it was Andrew who had "dark complexion, black hair, eyes" and it was Andrew, obviously who had the black habits—otherwise why would Mr. Selby have been willing to pay the reward for the return of Andrew alone, and not for the return of William alone?

It made no difference, however, because Mr. Selby did not get his apprentices back. They walked for several days, finally stopping in the town of Carthage, seventy-five miles southwest of Raleigh. There they decided to settle down for a time. Carthage was a small town, but there seemed to be room for a tailor shop. In two years as an apprentice, Andrew had learned enough to give him courage to try to strike out on his own. He took over a shack and advertised that he was establishing a tailoring business.

He seeemed to prosper in Carthage, but the town was too close to Raleigh for comfort. Until he was twenty-one years old, he could be seized and returned to Mr. Selby. He would also have to surrender everything he had acquired while working for himself. Under the law the master was bound to feed and clothe the apprentice and teach him the trade, and the apprentice was not allowed to accumulate property at his master's expense.

So, in the winter of 1824, Andrew Johnson left Carthage with his older but not wiser brother. Andrew was the leader, always. They went to Laurens, South Carolina. Andrew fell in love there, but the girl's family broke up the romance because he was a penniless tailor, and he left Laurens after a year or so.

Working on his own had not proved to be as satisfying as Andrew had hoped, and he had not learned as much as he thought he had learned in the two years of unwilling apprenticeship to Mr. Selby. He decided to go back and serve out the rest of his apprenticeship, but when Andrew arrived in Raleigh, he learned that Selby had moved twenty miles away. He walked to Selby's new shop and applied for forgiveness. Mr. Selby was willing to take Andrew back if Andrew would give him financial security—some valuables to make it worth while for Selby to teach Andrew, just in case the wanderlust struck him again. Andrew either did not have anything to give as security or his stubborn streak came out, for he did not do so. Instead he returned to Raleigh.

Raleigh was no place for Andrew to stay. Selby had a legal weapon to use against him at any time. If Andrew accumulated any money, or if he worked for another tailor, Selby could take the money because Andrew was an escaped runaway, still bound by the contract of indenture. So Andrew decided that he would leave North Carolina and head west, to see what he might make of his life in the backwoods country of Tennessee which was just opening up to settlement and business. He took along his mother and brother. They packed their possessions in a two-wheeled cart and set out for the West in August, 1826.

On the first day the party made thirty miles, alternately walking and riding, since there was not room in the cart for all of them. They stopped at Chapel Hill; then they started west, fording rivers and camping by the roadside or along the trail. They followed the Daniel Boone trail through the Blue Ridge country. It was adventurous travel all the way. One day Andrew and his brother killed a bear as they were hunting for meat for the family.

In September they reached the town of Greeneville, Tennessee, and decided to settle there. Andrew found work in the local tailor shop for a time, but he moved on to Rutledge, looking for a better opportunity, and stayed there until he learned that the Greeneville tailor had quit business. Then he returned to Greeneville, in March, 1827, and hung out a sign—"A. Johnson Tailor Shop." When Andrew opened the shop, he made a promise to himself: he would keep his own shop, he would never work for anyone else again, and he would never take a partner into his business. By the time he was nineteen years old, he had become fully independent in his thinking and thoroughly distrustful of other men. These were characteristics that he was to keep all his life, and they were to be a part of the story of his failure to achieve what he knew should be achieved in the Presidency.

In Tennessee, in 1827, it was possible for a young man without family or friends to aspire to high position and to wealth, but that is not to say that the ways of the South were not stamped on Greeneville. Long before Andrew Johnson and his family arrived in that town, a number of citizens of wealth had settled there. They selected the most favorable sites and built large, rambling houses on them. They accumulated more wealth and slaves, and they lived as did the other wealthy, upper-class families of the South, never soiling their hands with manual labor.

Andrew Johnson had no close relations with these people. His friends were the artisans and farmers of the area, men who felt free enough that they did not consider themselves of low estate, and who took politics seriously enough to argue about the important issues of the day with great concern. One debate in which Andrew Johnson engaged was on the subject of whether or not the criminal laws of Tennessee should be extended to cover the Tennessee Indians. He was a frequent and ardent debater, and thus, in spite of his lack of education, he gained a power of presentation and an ability to marshal arguments that were to help make him an effective politician.

In the autumn of 1826, Andrew resumed his search for education. He began attending public debates every Friday night at Greeneville College, a small school four miles out of town. At the same time he courted and married Eliza McCardle, the seventeen-year-old orphaned daughter of a Scotch shoemaker who had settled in Greeneville. Eliza taught Andrew to write. He was able to read a little at the time of their marriage but could only sign his mark as an

X. It took nearly ten years to give Andrew a passable hand, but as he studied, he also read all that he could and he educated himself to the extent that a solitary scholar could in a backwoods village early in the Nineteenth Century.

When they were married, Eliza and Andrew Johnson moved into a two-room building on Greeneville's main street. The front room was a tailor shop; the back room was kitchen, bedroom and parlor. The Johnsons lived there for four years, and Martha, their daughter, and Charles, the first son, were born there.

About four years after his marriage, Andrew's saving ways had enabled him to accumulate enough money to buy a real house to live in, and not long afterward they found a building for sale which could be used as a tailor shop. They bought it and moved it to the new lot, too.

Since Andrew Johnson was keenly interested in public affairs, and since he could easily do his work while talking with visitors, his shop became the center of village politics and gossip. He hired a reader and paid him fifty cents a day to read to him while he worked. The reader was given newspapers, speeches of politicians, and any books that could be found, and he droned them out to the tailor as he sat busily sewing at his bench.

Ever since anyone could remember, the aristocrats on the hill had been running public affairs in the town of Greeneville. In the spring of 1829, the aristocrats were astounded when they learned that Andy Johnson, the town tailor, was running for the position of alderman, and that he was supported by the mechanics and laboring men. He was elected, too, in spite of the harsh talk that went on behind the closed doors of the plantation houses. He served three terms as alderman, then three terms as mayor of the town.

When Andrew was twenty-five years old, he took part in calling a constitutional convention for the state of Tennes-

see. The object was to make the government more bearable
for the average man by abolishing imprisonment for debt,
and by removing the old property qualification for holding
public office which had made government the plaything of
the landed gentry in the past. Andrew Johnson, in other
words, was in the thick of the "revolution of the common
man" which was occurring in the western states in this
period.

First in Greeneville and then throughout the entire state
of Tennessee, Andrew Johnson became known as the leader
of the laboring classes. The mountaineers, who considered
themselves as good as any men alive, also came to regard him
as a leader who was concerned for their welfare.

In 1835, Andrew Johnson decided to run for the state
legislature to represent Washington and Greene Counties.
His opponent was Matthew Stephenson of Washington
County, a Whig. Johnson announced himself as a candidate
of the Democrats. In the beginning of the campaign Stephenson was given all the best of it by those who thought
they knew politics, for he was an experienced legislator,
while Andrew Johnson was a backwoods tailor with a smat-
tering of knowledge about public affairs gained through de-
bating and reading and listening in his shop.

The first debate between the candidates took place in
Washington County, Stephenson's home territory, where
Johnson was totally unknown. Stephenson led the discussion with talk about the Whig platform of internal improvements—roads and canals and other advantages to be built
by the federal government for the country's "general good."
The idea of the "general good" was not so strongly entrenched in America in the 1830's that it did not arouse
animosity. There were many men who believed that internal improvements meant centralized governmental control. The word Socialism was not used in those days, but
when Andrew Johnson answered Stephenson, he declared

that the curse of the times was too much legislation and too much government, and that the best governed nation was the least governed nation. "There are no good laws but such as repeal other laws," said Andrew Johnson.

Stephenson also said that he favored protection to home industry, (or high tariff), a national banking system and government paternalism. Andrew Johnson pointed out that there were no industries in east Tennessee that could benefit by high taxes. He spoke about Andrew Jackson's scuttling of the South Carolina scheme for nullification, or state's rights, and for the Union. He also spoke for retrenchment and economy in government. The anomaly of Johnson's position in favor of a Union, but not a very strong Union government, was lost on most of his listeners. The nation was not strongly in favor of centralized government. In fact, there was very little centralized government; the talk about this danger was good electioneering, but not far above the level of demagoguery.

There were other debates that year in both counties. Andrew comported himself very well, but possibly it was through his use of the magic name of Andrew Jackson, the hero of Tennessee, that he was able to win election by a narrow margin.

When he went to the Tennessee legislature in Nashville, Andrew Johnson was raw—there was no question about that. But he established himself there, too, as a champion of the people. He opposed public borrowing, high taxes, and all class legislation. He fought the idea of a state charter for a railroad on the grounds that it created a monopoly. He fought so hard against monopoly that he aroused the anger of many of the wealthy people of the state who had their fingers in various pies, and he was defeated for reelection to the lower house of the legislature. But in 1839, after one term out of office, he won election again.

By 1840, Andrew Johnson was well known throughout

Tennessee. That year he was chosen as one of the Democratic electors for the Presidential election. He was then a supporter of Martin Van Buren although he had not backed that New York Democrat in the previous election. In the campaign of 1840, Andrew Johnson earned a reputation as an orator, even though his ticket was defeated by the Whig candidates. But the defeat led to another Johnson victory—this time as state senator. He participated in some dark maneuvers, made necessary because of the division of the political parties in the two houses. In the House of Representatives in 1841, the Whigs held a majority of two seats. The Democrats had a majority of one in the Senate. So if a joint ballot was taken, the Whigs would have a majority of one. This became important when it came time to elect two United States senators, for in those days the senators were elected by the two houses of the state legislatures acting jointly.

Day after day the Whigs in the House voted to send the clerk of the House to the Senate, asking for a joint meeting to elect the two senators. A Whig member of the Senate, each time, arose and asked that a date be fixed for the meeting and election. Each time the motion was lost, for thirteen Democrats, led by Senator Johnson, voted Nay against the Ayes of twelve Whig senators.

When it became apparent, even to the stubborn Whigs, that no United States senators could be elected without compromise, Andrew Johnson and the other Democrats in the Senate told the Whigs their terms: they would agree to a joint session if the Whigs would let the Democrats elect one of the two senators.

On December 20, one of the Democratic senators submitted such a resolution. It lost, and as a result, no senators were selected by the Tennessee legislature at that session, and Andrew Johnson went down in local history as a member of the Immortal Thirteen, as they were known, who had blocked a Whig victory.

In this session of 1841, Andrew Johnson was involved in a movement to form a new state that would be composed of the mountain counties of Tennessee, North Carolina, Virginia, and Georgia. He was convinced that the people of these backwoods areas shared problems and attitudes that were not common to the states to which their areas belonged. Johnson's attitude was part of his basic sympathy for the laboring man, and this sympathy was the most important factor in his entire political life. If there was any man in the early part of the Nineteenth Century who could be called a "labor politician," it was Andrew Johnson of Tennessee. Earlier, and at this time as well, Johnson had opposed the various schemes for promoting internal improvements at public expense, even when these were to the apparent benefit of his mountaineer constituents. He had, for example, opposed a scheme for the building of macadamized roads throughout the state of Tennessee at taxpayers' expense, even though the roads would have helped his district. (This is one reason he was defeated in the election of 1837.) It can be said, therefore, that Johnson was a man of principle, not just a politician who blew with the wind to gain popular favor. But he was also a man of the laboring class, and he made sure that no one forgot it for a moment. In 1839, when he ran again for the state legislature after that first defeat, he once more opposed the internal improvements schemes and he also opposed the use of convict labor in competition with free labor. He referred to his Bible to convince his laboring-class contemporaries that many of the old Biblical characters were mechanics and artisans. Adam, he said, was a tailor who sewed fig leaves for clothing; Joseph, the husband of Mary, was a carpenter.

This way of thinking led Andrew Johnson to tour the

whole mountain area and in 1841, to propose the creation of a new state which was to be called Frankland. The mountain people owned very few slaves, if any, and did their own work with their own hands, quite unlike the majority of the white people of the plains. They were regarded by the lowland southerners as poor whites because they worked at manual labor. In the new state that Johnson sought to create, slaves would be restricted to ten per cent of the population and manual labor would be dignified as nowhere else in the land. No longer would wealth or family background make the man. The individual would be able to make his own way in the world.

Obviously, Andrew Johnson was something of a dreamer. He did not bother to project his dream into future generations to see if this "equality" could be maintained. In any case, the matter never went so far that such projection became important, for although Andrew was able to push the bill through the Tennessee Senate, it did not pass the House and was not heard of again.

Yet the same attitude that led Andrew Johnson to propose creation of a new state also led him to another strong position, one that was most important in his future career.

With the rise of slavery as a way of life in the southern states, the white southerners had adopted some practices that may seem astounding a century after the end of slavery, but which were accepted with scarcely a murmur in those days. Slaves were not considered to be people. While some Negroes were treated almost as human beings, if they worked in the household, legally they were pieces of property to be sold at the will of the master. They also occupied another peculiar legal niche: a Negro slave was counted as three-fifths of a human being for purposes of taxation and representation of a district in Congress and in state affairs. Of course no Negro could vote, and obviously no Negro could hold office, but politically at least they were part human.

This attitude was the cause of inequalities which angered Andrew Johnson and the mountain men of Tennessee and the other states. A county in the plains of western Tennessee, where the big plantations lay, might have a thousand white residents and fifteen thousand Negroes. A county in eastern Tennessee's mountains might have a population of 5,000 whites and only 1,500 Negro slaves. One would think, then, that for the purposes of elections the Tennessee mountain men would be able to control any vote where the two areas would be voting against one another. But that is not how it worked. The wealthy men of the South, who controlled the politics of the nation in its beginnings, established the constitution of the states and of the nation to provide that they would maintain control. A western Tennessee slave county, with its 1,000 whites and 15,000 slaves, would be given a population of 11,000; the eastern Tennessee white county, with its population of 5,000 whites and 1,500 slaves, would be given a population of only 6,000.

Because he felt so strongly about the rights of the laboring man, Andrew Johnson attacked this system when he became a member of the Senate of Tennessee. He proposed an amendment to the state constitution which would wipe out the three-fifths clause. In this way, control of state affairs would be placed in the hands of the majority of whites who voted and paid taxes.

This Johnson proposal was defeated in the Tennessee legislature, and it made the rich people of the South most suspicious of Johnson from that time on.

The wealthy men of Tennessee also suspected Andrew Johnson because he was outspoken and ill-educated. He could do something, and did, about his lack of education.

He collected all the political literature he could find, and stuffed scrapbooks full of clippings and articles from newspapers and other publications. But he made no attempt to hide his own beliefs about the class system in Tennessee. During one political campaign, an old enemy in Greeneville gave a party for everyone in town, to meet Johnson's rival. Naturally Andrew Johnson was not invited, but he was angry because he was not asked. Later, when he met someone who had attended the party, Andrew Johnson had strong words:

"Some day I will show the stuck-up aristocrats who is running the country," he said. "A cheap, purse-proud set they are, not half as good as the man who earns his bread by the sweat of his brow."

During most of the year, when the legislature was not in session, Andrew Johnson earned his way "by the sweat of his brow," working in his tailor shop. His exposure to political life had already brought him a measure of success. In 1842, sixteen years after he had settled in Greeneville, the Johnson tailor shop was as well established as any business in the community. He employed half a dozen journeymen tailors to do the work in the shop. Politics had not brought Andrew the love of the wealthy men of either the Whig or Democratic parties, but it had brought him financial success and the respect of the working people throughout his state.

He decided to run for Congress. His campaign would be based, as always, on sympathy for the working man and protection of the poor against the rich.

This program was not popular, any more than Andrew Johnson was, among the men who controlled the Tennessee Democratic Party. They objected violently to his candidacy. They were defeated, however, because Andrew Johnson held the loyalty of the people in his own district—or the working people who dominated that district. Yet that was not the end of the fight, for having lost the first round, the wealthy Democrats of the district joined the Whigs to put up another candidate, Colonel John Aiken. Colonel Aiken was a Democrat who lived in the town of Jonesboro. He represented the "quality" people of the region, and the Whigs were content to support him, for they knew they were unlikely to defeat the popular Andrew Johnson in an open partisan battle. The Colonel did not defeat Andrew Johnson, and the Whigs and dissident Democrats were never to defeat him until they became so outraged in 1851, that the enemy legislature rearranged (gerrymandered) the Congressional district so that voters who would oppose Johnson would control that area.

Following his election in 1842, Andrew Johnson went to Washington for the Twenty-eighth Congress. It was his first trip to the capital, which he found to be a huge city of 40,000. To a New Yorker or even a Richmond man of the day, Washington would not have been so impressive, but Tennessee was still very much frontier country. Greeneville, Andrew's home, had a population of less than a thousand, while Memphis, the largest town in the state, had a population of eight thousand. In the next two decades there would be huge changes in Washington, in Tennessee, and in the man who came to the nation's capital to represent the people of his state. But of all those changes, the least basic would be that in Andrew Johnson, whose principle of support for the common man was firmly established from his earliest days as a politician.

3 ☆

Ten Years in Congress

ANDREW Johnson followed the custom of the times and left his family living in their comfortable house in Greeneville while he took rooms in a boarding house on Capitol Hill. Only the wealthy could afford to bring their families so far, and only a brave congressman would dare to, for every two years he must go home and give his constituents an accounting of his actions in Congress.

Congressman Johnson went to Washington to work, and work he did. At his disposal was the growing Library of Congress, from which he borrowed books that more fortunate men had read in their school days: Plutarch's *Lives*, Aesop's *Fables*, and the works of Thomas Jefferson. When he was not occupied with the affairs of his district or those of the House, he studied or crossed over to the Senate to listen respectfully to the speeches of Henry Clay and other great orators. Clay might be a political enemy, but Johnson could learn from his enemies. Daniel Webster was out of the Senate, retired, when Johnson arrived in Washington, but Webster returned to the national capital shortly after, again to take up his post.

Andrew Johnson served in Congress at the same time that John Quincy Adams was there. He began his term as Adams was fighting against the famous "gag rule" which prevented

Congress from considering the petitions of citizens who wanted slavery abolished. Representative Johnson was wise enough to be quiet at first. His maiden speech in the House was made in favor of repayment to Andrew Jackson of a $1000 fine imposed on him when Jackson had been a general in charge of the occupation of New Orleans. Since Jackson had served as President, the resolution passed Congress quickly. Representative Johnson had been exposed to the House, and had acquitted himself properly. He could now be accepted as a serious member of Congress.

In his first term Andrew Johnson came up against old John Quincy Adams, but in a fashion that did not antagonize the one member of the House who had also been President of the United States. Johnson took the side of the South in the argument on the "gag rule," because the Constitution guaranteed the continuation of slavery, under the property clause.

John Quincy Adams had told a Massachusetts audience if slavery could only be abolished by war, then war should come. Andrew Johnson stood in the House, turned to the old Massachusetts man and asked him if, by advocating war, he was not violating the Constitution. John Quincy Adams, harried always by enemies more lustful, did not answer, but he did make note in his diary that the young Congressman from Tennessee had a great deal of native ability—a compliment worth cherishing, had Johnson but known of it.

Andrew Johnson created future trouble for himself in the winter of 1844, when an abolitionist named Joshua Giddings arose on the floor of the House to present a petition advocating the abolition of slavery in the District of Columbia. This was a favorite mark of the abolitionists; their position was that the District was a federal territory and that it thus did not come into the argument among the states. Southerners held that any attempt to abolish slavery in the District of Columbia was simply a forerunner for general abolition of slavery. They refused to consider abolition anywhere, anytime.

At this time—in 1844—in spite of Adams' struggle against the "gag rule," Congress would not hear petitions which called for abolition. If a congressman tried to bring one up, he was ruled out of order and told to sit down.

One day in January Joshua Giddings arose, and said he wanted to present a petition. No one took exception—the presentation of petitions signed by voters was common enough—it was only petitions relative to slavery that the Congress refused to hear.

But Giddings' petition did relate to slavery, and the following day the newspapers claimed that he had deceived the House by not so saying before he presented it.

The next day, Giddings arose to claim that he had been misrepresented. By this time tempers had been so aroused that the southern members of the House began shouting. Giddings claimed that he had announced the purpose of the petition, but that there had been so much noise on the floor of the House when he had risen to speak that no one had heard him. One congressman said that he had heard Giddings so state, but he was a northerner whose word was suspect among the southerners.

A struggle developed when Giddings asked for "personal privilege"—the right of a congressman to defend himself against attack. If he was to have the right of personal privilege on this question, the rules of the House would have to be suspended temporarily, and this could be accomplished only by a two-thirds vote. When the vote came, Andrew Johnson, alone among southern congressmen, voted to give Giddings a chance to speak. For years after, Johnson's enemies were to cite this as proof positive that Andrew Johnson was really an abolitionist in disguise.

In this first term in Congress, Johnson was also involved in the disputes over the annexation of Texas and the Oregon question. To Johnson this was one question, for it had been posed as one question by the Democrats in their platform of 1840. At that time it had been agreed that Texas would come into the Union as a slave state, and Oregon would be admitted as a free state. But while Texas was to be annexed to the Union in 1845, with southern and northern votes, the southerners decided to abandon the party platform in the case of Oregon. Combined with British claims against the territory, this was enough to prevent the entrance of Oregon into the Union at that time.

These struggles occurred under the Whig administration of John Tyler, who had succeeded William Henry Harrison to the Presidency a month after Harrison's inauguration. In the election to come, Tyler wanted to run, but Henry Clay won the Whig nomination, and James K. Polk, former Governor of Tennessee, became the candidate of the Democratic Party. The questions of Texas and Oregon were the vital issues of the campaign, and although Polk failed to carry his own state, he was elected.

In the Congressional election of 1844, Andrew Johnson was opposed by William G. Brownlow, a Whig who was also a minister of the Gospel. National issues came into the campaign; so did religion—Johnson was accused of being a Roman Catholic and also of being an infidel who believed in nothing. The charges did not help Parson Brownlow's cause. Johnson was elected by more than twice his previous margin. He won by 1300 votes, which was a comfortable victory, and an especially good victory for a Democrat in that section of Tennessee at that time.

Andrew Johnson's second term as congressman was important to his career in later life, for it was in this second term, in 1846, that he introduced the Homestead Bill. Once again, his interest in this particular legislative idea was sparked by his concern for the working man. His Homestead Bill was intended to help the plebeian.

At that time, before the Civil War, the area that lies between the Mississippi River and the Rocky Mountains was very sparsely settled. Much of the land had come to the United States as part of the Louisiana Purchase, and was thus government land. Land was plentiful, and settlers were needed to expand and consolidate the national boundaries and the territory that lay between them. As Congressman Johnson noted in one of his early speeches on the subject, the government owned three quarter-sections of land, or 480 acres, for every voter in the country.

Johnson proposed that the public lands of the United States be opened to the people, and that a quarter-section be given to any person who would settle on it for five years and cultivate it, build a house on it, and improve it. That meant that a man could aspire to ownership of 160 acres if he was willing to move there to live.

Southern congressmen opposed the bill, because they were opposed to the settlement of land in territories closed to slavery. Further, even had the territories not been closed, they would have opposed the scattering of independent, non-slaveholding whites across the country. The southerners wanted slavery preserved at any cost.

So the Homestead Bill came up year after year in Congress, and was defeated year after year. Not during his tenure as congressman was Andrew Johnson to see the bill become a law.

Congressman Johnson was to remain a representative until 1851. During that period he was to become well known in the House and in the nation as the defender of the common man. His handwriting might lack the niceties of those trained in the universities and by private tutors; his rhetoric might lack polish, but his strength and sincerity carried him through.

At one point he debated hotly with Jefferson Davis on the question of increasing appropriations for the United States Military Academy at West Point. Johnson claimed that it was wasteful to spend so much money in employing high-priced "experts" to teach there.

"Can a blacksmith or a tailor construct the bastioned fieldworks opposite Matamoros?" Davis asked grandly, referring to a point on the Mexican-Texas border.

Johnson grew angry.

"I am a mechanic," he said, "and when a blow is struck, on that class I will resent it. I know we have an illegitimate, swaggering, bastard, scrub aristocracy which assumes to know a great deal, but which, when the flowing veil of pretension is torn off from it, is seen to possess neither talents nor information on which one can rear a useful superstructure. . . ."

These were harsh words, and they were harshly taken. Later, when Johnson sought to extend an olive branch of friendship to Davis, the southern aristocrat would have none of it.

Johnson was a man of the people in a way that few could match. He never forgot that he was born in poverty and grew up without care or education. His upbringing and status, until he was well into his teens, were not unlike those of the slaves; he understood better than most men just how close to slavery were the freemen without property, and he fought always to improve their chances in a nation where in the 1840's and 1850's freedom was a relative term.

In many ways Johnson would be regarded by later standards as anything but a "progressive" congressman. He voted against establishment of the Smithsonian Institution, and when it was established, he tried to change that historic museum and incubator of science into a school for training American mechanics in the various trades. He voted against appropriations to add to the space of the United States Patent Office, claiming that the patent office was largely a fraud. He had earlier voted against macadamized roads and against the establishment of a railroad in his own Tennessee. In Congress he showed no more foresight in matters that related to the general good.

But as protector of the working class he had no peer. If others wanted high tariffs to protect industry, Johnson wanted low ones to protect the man who bought goods in the open market. When others moved to increase the pay of government employees, Johnson tacked a rider on the bill which would make sure that the pay of the man with pick and shovel was also increased. He wanted to decrease the pay of congressmen and cut down the number of government employees, since, he said, they were "mere henchmen and fuglemen, going around the country blowing the horn of their bosses." While other congressmen banded together in a protective club, Representative Johnson complained of waste and mismanagement of funds. He knew one congressman, he said, who had disposed of books and stationery which belonged to the government, selling goods worth $500 for $150 to put in his own pocket.

He did not like public debt, or cities, or the rabble who lived in them and squeezed out a living by means Johnson would not have termed honest work. As an advocate of honesty and economy in government he practiced what he preached; on one occasion he returned to the government $216 which, he said, was overpayment on an allowance for travel and mileage.

This attitude of saving and this suspicious view of government has never been known to make a congressman popular with his fellows. Johnson had many enemies in Congress because of his forthright attacks on what he considered to be abuses of the public purse. And so, as were many others who had enemies, he was accused of drunkenness and carousing, and his rough speech and rough ways were set down as the outward signs of a man of no worth. This was not unusual: Henry Clay had much the same experience; Daniel Webster was also victim of much animosity. But they were men of an earlier generation who were bearing such attacks just now. The assault on Johnson was to come in force much later.

There was nothing of the prude about Johnson, and from time to time he drank more than was good for him—but so did many men in those days, some of them men in very high places.

Also, although he struggled with Jefferson Davis over such issues as the Homestead Bill, Andrew Johnson was basically a southerner. He owned ten slaves himself. He was disliked not for his appearance or his "crudeness," for actually he dressed very well and his manners, if not those of a man born to gentility, were at least those of a man of dignity. No, Johnson was disliked by the Whigs everywhere because, by his own claim, he was a man of the common people. He advocated laws that would help the laboring men and artisans—laws like a lien law which made it possible for an artisan either to collect for his work or attach the property of the landholder. As he said himself, he opposed the system of capitalism which grew up in the twenty or thirty years just before the Civil War, and which was to create the age of the Robber Barons—the Vanderbilts, Goulds, Fiskes, and others who created monopoly and turned it into license. Johnson blamed the Whig Party for this development.

He was also disliked by southern politicians as time went on, because they feared his Homestead Bill, and although he was himself a slaveowner, they did not believe that he stood solidly behind the perpetuation of slavery. The last straw

for the southerners was the passage by the House of Representatives of Johnson's Homestead Bill in the spring of 1852.

Two years before, in 1850, Henry Clay had returned to the
Senate and to history by drawing up and pushing through a
compromise on the issue of slavery and the new territories
that postponed a violent confrontation of the opposing
forces on the problem caused by slavery. The compromise
contained a number of provisions; not all of them related to
slavery, but that was the major issue. California would come
into the Union as a free state, but in exchange for this con-
cession there would be no restriction on slavery in the organization of the remaining territory acquired from Mexico
(New Mexico, parts of Utah, Nevada, Arizona, and Colo-
rado). It also provided that there would be no interference
with slavery in the District of Columbia, but that the slave
trade would end there. Congress would not interfere in
interstate slave trade, and there would be more effective
laws for the return of fugitive slaves.

As such, there was no Compromise of 1850. This term
refers to five laws that were passed to accomplish the above.
For a time it appeared that the compromises had taken the
poison out of American political life—but only for a few
months. Later that same year abolitionists began rescuing
escaped slaves. True, there were not many cases, but the
existence of the Underground Railroad infuriated the
South, and the actions taken by abolitionists to keep from
returning slaves made the southerners fear that the constitutional guarantees of the "right" of slavery were in danger.

So, when Andrew Johnson's Homestead Act was passed
by the House of Representatives in the spring of 1852, southerners were seriously worried lest northern whites and
whites from the border regions who had small use for
slavery, would enter the new territories covered by the
Compromise of 1850 and would turn them into free terri-

tories. It would not take many such changes to upset the balance of power in Congress; once this occurred the South feared it would be only a matter of time until the northerners destroyed the South's way of life.

Johnson's Homestead Act was delayed and finally died in the Senate for that session, but when he came home to Tennessee at the end of the Congressional season, his enemies decided that he was too dangerous and must be removed.

The Whigs controlled the legislature of Tennessee in 1852, and they simply legislated Andrew Johnson out of office. They did it by cutting his home county off from the First District, which was the Congressional district in which he had won so many elections. His Greene County was attached to the Second District, which had much more population and was overwhelmingly Whig in sentiment. In so doing, his enemies thought they had disposed of Andrew Johnson.

Johnson thought so too for a time. He was embittered and declared that he was going to give up politics and devote himself to business from that time on.

4 | ☆

Gerrymandered Into the Governor's Chair

L̲ATE in 1852, still smarting from his wounds, Andrew Johnson told Democratic friends that he would be available if they wished to nominate him to run against the incumbent Whig governor, W. B. Campbell. A few months later he had selected his campaign manager and was ready to make the fight.

Had Governor Campbell chosen to remain in office, it might have been an historic struggle, because Campbell was the strongest man among the Tennessee Whigs. But Campbell refused to run for a third term, and the Whigs were forced to look elsewhere.

They chose Gustavus A. Henry, known across the state as the Eagle Orator. He was the man who had maneuvered Andrew Johnson out of office by working out the gerrymandering scheme, and there could not have been a candidate that Andrew would have preferred to defeat, if that was possible.

In five Congressional campaigns Andrew Johnson had earned a reputation as a hard man to go against in debate. A newspaper reporter from New York, who had heard him campaigning, said that he cut and slashed about him with

such effort that "he tore big wounds and left something behind to fester and be remembered." This writer noted that
Johnson's phraseology might be "uncouth" and his way of
talking crude, but it was easy for the crowds to understand
him, and he had something to say. He had no fear of insult
either given or taken; he asked for no gentle treatment and
gave none.

Election campaigns in the backwoods country of Tennessee in the 1840's and 1850's were not for weaklings. In
one campaign, that against Parson Brownlow, the Parson
charged that Johnson was an illegitimate child, son of the
cashier of the bank in which old Jacob Johnson had been
porter. Johnson was so angry with that foul charge that
after he had won the election he made a special trip to
Raleigh just to get the facts and disprove the false claim.
His enemies were "ghouls and hyenas," he said.

When Johnson discovered that Gustavus Henry was to be
his opponent, he laid his plans for the campaign. The word
'gerrymander' was coined in 1812 when Governor Elbridge
Gerry of Massachusetts had created a new district, so mis-
shapen that it looked like a salamander, to make sure of
electing a Republican to office. The people called the trick
district a 'gerrymander' and the name stuck.

The first time that Andrew Johnson and Gustavus Henry
met in public discussion during the campaign, Johnson
made use of that information. "Fellow Citizens," he said,
"the Whigs have cheated me out of Congress, they have
torn the county of Greene from its sister counties, and attached it to a lot of foreign counties. They have split it up
till it looks like a salamander. The fact is, they have 'gerrymandered' me out of Congress—no, I am mistaken, they
have not 'gerrymandered' me out, they have 'Henryman-
dered' me out!"

Henry was an experienced politician, too. He met John-

son in an Irish district, and brought up a vote cast by
Congressman Johnson against a resolution to make an appropriation from the federal treasury to send aid to famine-
stricken Ireland. Johnson admitted that he had voted against
the bill. He did not believe that the Congress had the right
to spend federal money for such purposes.

"But," he added, "I proposed to the members that we give
our salaries for a certain length of time and when they
would not agree to this, I put my hand in my pocket and
gave fifty dollars to the cause. How much did you give?" he
asked his opponent.

"Nothing," said Gustavus Henry, as the crowd jeered.

It was a close election. Johnson won by 2,500 of 124,000
votes.

He took the oath of office on October 3, 1853, in the new
state capitol at Nashville. He came into office in a period
that was difficult both for Tennessee and the Union. Perhaps
the split in Tennessee showed just how difficult it was. In
that state, in 1853, a new United States senator was to be
selected. But so divided were the political feelings of the
voters, and thus of the legislature, that forty-nine ballots
were taken before the lawmakers agreed on John Bell, a
Whig who would desert the fold and become the Presidential candidate of the Constitutional Union Party in
1860.

Between Whig and Democrat were several fundamental
differences, most important of which was the Whig contention that the nation needed a strong federal government,
and the Democratic belief that he who governs least, governs
best. The new Governor dwelt on these issues in an inaugural address that was regarded by his friends as the finest
message ever to come from his pen, and by his enemies as a
stewpot filled with empty rhetoric.

But having made a highly emotional inaugural address,

Governor Johnson settled down to attend to specific details of government in his message to the state legislature. The program he outlined called for extension of popular education, to be supported by general public taxation. He asked the legislature to instruct its senators and representatives to work for passage of the Homestead Bill. He asked that the legislature inaugurate a bill to elect the President and Vice-President of the United States by popular vote, rather than by the indirect method of the Electoral College.

These were such advanced ideas that the conservatives of the western part of Tennessee charged that Johnson was a representative of the interests of northern labor, who was leading the rabble against its betters. But the more the wealthy of the state abused Johnson, the more he appealed to the poor people, who crossed party lines to vote for him.

Toward the end of his first term, in 1855, Johnson sought renomination as governor and was again chosen—but not by all the leaders of the Democratic party in Tennessee. Indeed, the committee on resolutions, which represented the traditional elements within the party, came forth with a strong resolution in favor of the party's national program, including support of President Franklin Pierce, but managed only a watered-down resolution in support of Governor Johnson.

While in Nashville, Andrew Johnson took rooms at a hotel, rather than move his family from their home in Greeneville. The home was a new one, a handsome brick house on Main Street which he had purchased in 1851, along with a surrounding acre of land. Charles, one of Johnson's sons, was a physician. Robert, the other, was a student of law and would be a lawyer. Both boys would die early. One of his two daughters, Mary, would marry a judge, and the other would marry a distant connection of Abraham Lincoln.

Even then Andrew Johnson was accused of scandalous behaviour while away from home. The imputation was made—and often—that he drank to excess and caroused with women. But these were not unusual charges in the Tennessee of the 1850's. The same charges were made over in Kentucky against Henry Clay. Each man's enemies chose to believe the charges of wrongdoing implicitly, and his friends to reject them totally. Out of the election campaigns came such diverse pictures of the candidates and men who have since become national heroes that it is difficult to separate truth from fiction.

One thing is certain: liquor consumption in Tennessee and throughout the South in the 1850's was high. Andrew Johnson, like Henry Clay, was not priggish, and he drank to excess on occasion. It was difficult not to do so, for at political stump meetings and dinners the whiskey barrel was always out and open, and the fiery liquor passed around. Drinking was part of southern politics. It was, also, known as the "curse of the South" for the careers of many young men, including Johnson's two sons, were brought to early ends by excessive drinking.

In 1856, while Andrew Johnson's star was rising, that of old Henry Clay was waning in the land. His Whig Party was dissolving. In the North it was giving way to the new Republican movement. In the South, many Whigs turned to a party called the American, or Know Nothing Party, which was particularly strong that year in Tennessee, probably because of the settlement there of a considerable Irish community.

The American Party's slogan was "American for Americans." To a great extent it was simply anti-Catholic. A section of the party's bylaws read that a member must be a native-born citizen of the United States, a Protestant, either born of Protestant parents or raised as a Protestant, and he could not be married to a Roman Catholic. Another section read thus:

"Are you willing to use your influence and vote for native-born American citizens for all offices of honor, trust, and profit in the gift of the people, to the exclusion of all foreigners and aliens, and Roman Catholics in particular, and without regard to party predilection?"

The growth of this American Party was not the cause of anti-Catholicism in America, but it was certainly a symptom of the reaction to the wave of immigrants from Catholic lands and the clannishness they naturally exhibited in a new country which made the immigrants a powerful political force.

The party became known as the Know Nothing Party because of the reticence of its members to discuss their political strength or ideas. When outsiders asked questions of members of the semi-secret society, they replied "I don't know." The name was an obvious consequence of such behaviour.

In Andrew Johnson's second campaign for the governorship in 1856, he ran against Meredith P. Gentry, a former congressman and a skillful orator. Gentry was the candidate of the Whigs and Know Nothings, who combined against Johnson and in reaction to Henry Clay and the Kansas-Nebraska Act of 1854, which threatened slavery by leaving the question up to the people who settled in these territories.

The Kansas-Nebraska Act was officially a major issue between Governor Johnson and former Congressman Gentry, but the private lives of the candidates figured importantly as well. His opponent charged that Johnson's daughter had been educated in a convent at Georgetown, Maryland, although the poor girl, Martha, had actually studied at Mrs. English's Seminary for Young Ladies in that town.

It was another close election; the governor won by just over 2100 votes of 130,000. And once again, Johnson de-

voted himself to the problems of state administration. It was
a second conservative administration in fiscal matters, but
again a liberal one in social and economic affairs. The governor was responsible for the purchase of Andrew Jackson's
old home, The Hermitage, as a state historic site. He persuaded the legislature to appropriate money for agricul-
tural and mechanical fairs, further showing his dedication
to the working man of city and farm. He also persuaded the
state legislature to appropriate money for expansion of the
state library, to employ a state librarian who would buy
books, arrange them, and supervise their use. In a way, this
was a beginning for Tennessee, since the state was new and
raw and had little interest in the cultural affairs deemed so
important in the cities of the East.

Governor Johnson was not popular with the national
leaders of the Democratic Party, particularly those in the
South. President Polk had sneered at Johnson's Homestead
Bill. The Calhoun-Davis group of fiery leaders held him in
contempt as "not a gentleman." In Tennessee in the 1850's,
one did not have to be a gentleman to succeed in politics.
But plain talk, even in Tennessee, sometimes led to serious
consequences, for Tennessee's gentlefolk were southern
through and through, and brought with them to the state the
southern habit of settling quarrels by violence. Men were
forever trying to force Andrew Johnson into duels; he did
not believe in dueling and would have no part of it and
this caused much sneering among the "gentlemen" about his
courage.

After his second election as governor, Andrew Johnson
went to Nashville to attend a victory celebration. But the
Whigs and Know Nothings decided to break up the party
and massed in the back of the hall. When Governor Johnson appeared to speak, they set up a loud clamor, so that the

speakers could scarcely be heard in the hall. Johnson was furious. He began to read the secret political oath of the Know Nothings. "Such a person," he said, "is not a free man but a slave, and his liberty is controlled by a Know Nothing conclave."

As Johnson spoke those words, T. T. Smiley, a Whig, came to the platform and asked the governor to moderate his language, because Smiley had worked with the Know Nothings, and he and other Whigs could take the language as a personal affront.

The governor refused. He denounced those who would try to muzzle him and spoke more harshly than ever.

Smiley then challenged the governor to a duel, but friends reasoned with the two men. Smiley admitted that he was not at the meeting to break up Johnson's speech, but to keep the Whigs in control. Johnson said that he was not referring directly to Smiley, but to those who were trying to wreck the meeting. The duel was avoided.

Generally speaking, Andrew Johnson got on well with the state legislature, although for a time the Senate was controlled by the Whigs. He was a strong executive, but he had served in the legislature and as a congressman, so he respected the rights of the legislators as well as those of the governor. And his constant concern for the people of the state, as opposed to the wealthy landowners, brought him a broad support.

In four years back in Tennessee, after ten years in Washington, Andrew Johnson had done what he set out to do. He had cemented his leadership and political power, and had made himself the most powerful leader in the state. So in the fall of 1857, as the issue of slavery mounted above all others in the affairs of the nation, Andrew Johnson decided that he would again seek national office, and placed himself as can-

didate for the United States Senate seat vacated by James C.
Jones. On the first ballot he received fifty-seven votes to his
opponent's thirty-eight, and thus it was decided that Andrew
Johnson would be the junior United States senator from
Tennessee. It was, he said, the achievement of his highest
ambition.

5 | ☆

In the Senate

THEY called him "the bound boy of Raleigh" when they wanted to insult Senator Andrew Johnson, but his associates respected him none the less, and when he went to take his seat in the United States Senate in the Thirty-fifth Congress, they offered him the chairmanship of a special committee on government expenditures.

This was done in recognition of Johnson's interest in financial affairs and his insistence that government spending be kept at a minimum. But Johnson was also a traditionalist. He refused the special appointment, saying that the work ought to be done by the Judiciary Committee or another regular committee of the Senate.

Almost immediately, Senator Johnson was pitted against Senator Jefferson Davis of Mississippi, one of the leaders of the slavery bloc. The antagonism was not entirely over slavery, but over basic differences in concept of the function of the federal government. Senator Davis advocated a large standing army, and was joined in that advocacy by most of the Democratic senators. The Republicans feared the idea, because they believed that under a Democratic administration the army would be used to further the cause of slavery in the territories. Andrew Johnson aligned himself with the northern Republicans against the slave states and earned the increased enmity of Jefferson Davis.

Senator Johnson annoyed Davis and others because he opposed the building of the Union Pacific Railroad, insisting that this was the job of private business and not that of the Congress. He locked horns with other southern senators on several issues.

The most important issue of those days, dwarfing all others, was slavery, which came before Congress many times in many ways. In February, 1858, the issue was presented to the Senate in the Lecompton Constitution of Kansas, which sought to become admitted to the Union as a state. This constitution would have made Kansas a slave state for all practical purposes. Senator John Bell of Tennessee, Johnson's senior colleague, voted against the acceptance of this constitution, while Johnson favored it. The Tennessee legislature then called on Senator Bell to resign for betraying the interests of his state and slavery. Bell answered, and Andrew Johnson felt impelled to reply in turn to Bell. This interchange led to a breach between Bell and Johnson which was never to be healed. It also showed the feeling of the people of Tennessee—or at least of the people who sat in the legislative chambers in Nashville.

The talk of secession grew loud and constant in 1859, so much so that in December the House of Representatives did not even adjourn for the usual Christmas holidays. Two issues had inflamed the legislators of North and South. One was the John Brown raid on Harper's Ferry. The southerners said this could not have come about without northern —and thus Republican—support. They were almost equally furious with John Sherman, the leading candidate for the speakership of the House. This Ohio legislator had endorsed a book called *The Impending Crisis*, by Hinton Rowan Helper, a poor white from North Carolina. Helper made the case that slavery was killing the South, not because it was morally wrong, but because it was economically wrong, wasteful, and expensive.

From the moment of its opening, it was apparent to all Washington that this Thirty-sixth Congress had but one subject for debate: slavery. Mrs. Roger A. Pryor, wife of a southern statesman and legislator and one of the most acceptable of Washington matrons of the time, wrote that "it was evident from the first hour that the atmosphere was heavily charged." Former President Tyler, retired on his plantation, wrote: "I fear the debate in Congress, and above all the Speaker's election. If excitement prevails in Congress, it will add fuel to the flame which already burns so terrifically."

Excitement did prevail, and the fires were fanned. Mrs. Pryor's husband, a representative from Virginia, challenged Representative Potter of Wisconsin to a duel, so heated had their arguments become. Potter chose bowie knives, but Pryor refused to engage in so barbarous a method of dueling.

Senator Johnson began to consult Helper's book, for the sentiments it expressed were not unlike his own. But Andrew Johnson did not truly believe the Union to be in danger in 1860, as the Senate reconvened after the holidays. He had heard the threats that if Abraham Lincoln was elected there would be secession, but he paid them no more attention than he had the threats of secession four years before. Johnson did not agree with John C. Calhoun and Jefferson Davis, who held that every state had the right to take itself out of the Union if it found the laws passed by the federal Congress to be hateful. He agreed with Daniel Webster in interpreting the opening words of the Constitution of the United States. Those two said that the words: "We the people of the United States . . ." showed that the designers of the Constitution had intended to make the people of the nation, not the states of the Union, sovereign. The people were sovereign through the work of their national representatives in Congress and the federal government.

Over ten years the position of the southerners in Congress had changed significantly. Earlier, they had taken a stand against the right of Congress to legislate slavery out of the territories controlled by the federal government. There were many men, including Andrew Johnson, who saw fair argument in that position. But weakened by the growth of the North and the sterility and feebleness of the South's economy, the legislators of the South went further. They saw their own position, and they became emboldened by desperation, realizing that if affairs continued as they had in the 1840's and early 1850's, the days of slavery were numbered.

So under Jefferson Davis and a handful of other leaders, the southerners took the position that Congress *must* legislate to keep slavery in the territories. This was a position announced by Davis in a group of resolutions on February 29, 1860.

The Democrats were to meet in convention in Charleston in April, and many of them from the South believed that Davis's action was aimed at preventing the nomination of Stephen A. Douglas of Illinois, the logical and almost certain Democratic candidate, because Douglas was known to favor the right of the settlers to make their own decision. Much as he might have been opposed to Douglas, Senator Davis had a deeper motive. It was to make certain that either the candidate or the Democratic Party platform came out squarely to protect the rights of slaveowners in the territories which were governed by the federal authorities. In other words, he and the other leaders of the South were determined that slavery should not be outlawed anywhere in the North American continent where state action had not already outlawed it.

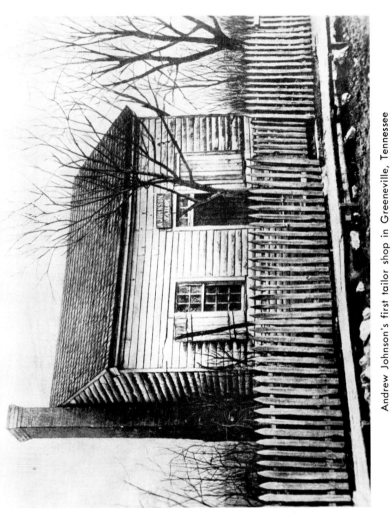

Andrew Johnson's first tailor shop in Greeneville, Tennessee

Andrew Johnson taking the oath of office in the Kirkwood House

President Johnson pardoning former Confederates after the Civil War

President Johnson on his ill-fated 1866 tour of the country

Thaddeus Stevens closing the debate on impeachment in the House

The Senate as a Court of Impeachment for the trial of Andrew Johnson

President Johnson being served with the summons to appear before the high court of impeachment

Cartoon of 1869 predicting Johnson's return to the clothing business

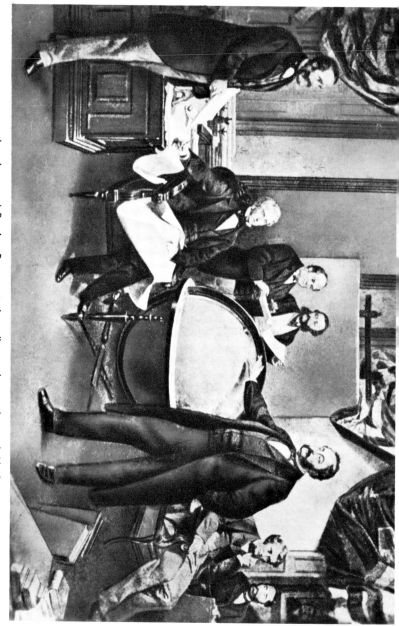

American and Russian Representatives discuss the purchase of Alaska

Many unsuspecting Democrats were gulled by the apparently simple, personal political motives of Davis and his friends. President Buchanan, who had no use for Douglas, thought this was the motive. Andrew Johnson thought so too. Shrewder observers, however, realized that this was a kill-or-cure move by the die-hards of slavery who realized that one must disrupt the Democratic Party before the clear issue could be raised, or rally the party and win the day for slavery.

Senator Johnson's major concern in the winter and spring of 1860, was not the slavery issue, as such, although it bore upon it, but his Homestead Bill, which had never passed both houses of Congress. He had no interest in the Davis resolutions, and believed that they were unimportant, since it was conceded by nearly all southerners that all the lands in the west where slavery would be economically sound, had already been given statehood. So why should anyone worry about so impractical a matter, Johnson wondered? Still, he voted with the South, as did nearly all the Democrats, when the resolutions were brought before the Senate. Probably he did so in a trade of votes for his Homestead Bill.

As a southerner, a slave-owner, and yet a man of the common people, Andrew Johnson was of differing feelings about the position of his more strident southern acquaintances. He saw no way to handle the Negro except through slavery:

"If you liberate the Negro," he asked, "what will be the next step? . . . What will we do with two million negroes in our midst? . . . You can't get rid of the Negro except by holding him in slavery."

Yet Senator Johnson also believed that "preservation of the Union ought to be the object that is paramount to all other considerations." Apparently, Johnson had some hope, at least, of being nominated at the Charleston convention for the Presidency. The hope vanished at Charleston, and when the Democrats adjourned there and then met again at Baltimore, he asked that his name not be presented. He believed at that time that his greater duty lay in an attempt to preserve the Union.

Between the two conventions, Johnson's Homestead Bill had been passed by both houses of Congress, only to be vetoed by President Buchanan. It would be two more years, after the South had left the Union, before the bill would become a law.

The defeat of his favorite piece of legislation put Andrew Johnson in a lonely position. He had been deserted by his own leadership, and while he was not unused to playing a lone political hand, still his position was an uncomfortable one in the summer of 1860. He went home to Tennessee, to be surprised by old friends who had suddenly turned secessionist—if a Republican candidate were elected to the Presidency.

The South's William L. Yancey came to Tennessee that summer, talking secession. Where did Johnson stand? Eventually, during the campaign, he went speech-making around his state in favor of John C. Breckinridge, the southern Democrats' candidate for the Presidency. He was not an effective speaker, particularly in the west and central part of the state where the secessionist movement was strong. He spoke always of Breckinridge as a Union man who would not destroy the Union; he cut the words Black Republican out of his speeches about Abraham Lincoln, and he did nothing to further the popular, but quite untrue, belief that the South was strong and growing stronger while the North was weak and growing weaker.

In Memphis, Andrew Johnson was asked the question that interested every man in the border states:

"What do you advise, Senator Johnson, if Lincoln is elected?"

"As for myself," replied Johnson, "I shall stay inside the Union and there fight for southern rights. I advise all others to do the same."

When election day came, and Abraham Lincoln was chosen as President of the United States, Andrew Johnson faced a supreme choice, one more difficult for him than for most men of the day. The die-hard southerners welcomed the election returns as showing them that they must dissolve the Union and go it alone. The northerners welcomed the returns, as showing that the Union would not be dissolved. Andrew Johnson must choose a side. He could not choose the side of the South, under which his Homestead principle would be forever dead, and under which the artisan could never aspire to become a full-fledged citizen. On the day before the election Col. J. J. Turner of Gallatin invited Johnson to tea, and while there, the Senator predicted that Lincoln would be elected and that the South would attempt to secede. As for himself, he said, he would stand by the Union. He intended to return to Washington and come out against secession. The attempt to secede would fail in any event, he said.

Colonel Turner telegraphed the governor of Tennessee and Senator Nicholson, the other United States senator, and at Nashville all of them tried to persuade Andrew Johnson to declare himself for the South. They had no success. Andrew Johnson had decided to stand alone.

Much of the North, and many northern congressmen, were shocked by the actual declarations of secession from the leaders of the South, and even more shocked at the secession convention called by South Carolina. Once it became apparent that the South was bent on leaving the Union, some northerners counseled that the Union should, in Horace Greeley's words, "let the erring sisters go in peace." Very few congressmen felt strongly about maintaining the Union

—certainly not strongly enough to go to war about it. Many of the abolitionists were happy to see the South go and thus to eliminate slavery from the ranks of the states of the Union. Had there been no men like Abraham Lincoln and Andrew Johnson in the United States, the Confederacy would have become an established fact, and today the people of the old Union might be living in two or more nations.

On December 18, 1860, the senators from South Carolina announced that their state was withdrawing from the Union. The word was greeted with shouts and angry voices. Many men in the Senate were armed, and pistols flashed on the floor that day. Amid the noise and confusion, Senator Andrew Johnson arose and gained the floor. He was a southern senator, and so not all those in the room were aware of his feelings about secession. Also, some on the side of withdrawal hoped that he had been persuaded to change his mind. Far from that, he had that very morning received word from Tennessee that a convention of the leading citizens of his mountain country had met a few days before and had backed his belief that secession was unthinkable. They had not gone quite that far, actually, but had said that secession was unthinkable until every means of compromise had been tried out. But that was enough for Andrew Johnson, if he needed outside prompting.

Johnson announced that he proposed to pursue a resolution he had introduced five days before, amending the Constitution so that if the nation elected a northern President it must elect a southern Vice-President. The indications, as he spoke, were that he was a southern senator with a full and hearty belief in the differences between the two regions of the nation.

But as he went on, Senator Johnson disproved that assumption. He did so in five short words:

"I am opposed to secession. . . ." he said.

With that announcement an angry murmur began in the gallery, which was that day filled with southerners. Washington was and is a southern city by nature, and on December 18, 1860, the wives and families of many of the southern senators were in the gallery, knowing that they were witnessing historic moments.

Senator Johnson ignored the murmurs.

"If the doctrine of secession is to be carried out upon the mere whim of a state, this government is at an end! No state has a right to secede from this Union without the consent of the other states which ratified the compact!"

The noise grew louder, but Senator Johnson did not stop. He had waited for this moment and prepared for it.

He charged the North with wrongdoing in enacting Liberty Laws which contradicted the Constitution and federal laws. He charged that the South was acting with equal impropriety in trying to back out of the contract of Union.

He was assailed by a Vermont senator because he had named Vermont as one of the wrongdoing northern states. He was assailed by many southern senators, who grew sharp and acid in their personal attacks on him.

"What is this issue?" he demanded. "It is this and only this: we are mad because Mr. Lincoln has been elected and we have not got our man. If we had got our man, we should not be for breaking up the Union, but as Mr. Lincoln *is* elected, we are breaking up the Union. Am I to be so great a coward as to retreat from duty? No sirs! Here I will stand and meet the encroachments upon my country at the threshold!"

There were many interruptions. It took Andrew Johnson all the rest of that day's session and much of that of the next afternoon to complete his speech. When it was ended, there was no applause. From the galleries came taunts, and from the floor southern sympathizers followed him into the cloakroom, and from the Capitol to his rooms at Kirkwood House, goading, insulting, shouting at him to duel or fight with them.

That night, as Andrew Johnson remained in his rooms and wrote a long letter home to his wife in Greeneville, in the hotel rooms and saloons and lobbies of the town his name was in nearly every conversation. Reports of his speech were transmitted to California and to every corner of the nation.

What was the effect of the Johnson speech? Alexander H. Stephens, who became vice-president of the Confederate States of America, said after the war was long past that had it not been for Andrew Johnson, the South would have achieved her independence without war. Johnson, said Alexander Stephens, had rallied the people of the North to the principle of union.

Had there been no Andrew Johnson, perhaps there would have been another to rise during that day or the one after. Abraham Lincoln, assuredly, would not have given up as so many northern congressmen were prone to do. But Johnson was there, to make his speech, and stir a quiescent Union to life.

6 ☆

Turncoat or Hero?

THE most vicious attacks against Andrew Johnson in the Senate were leveled by General Joseph Lane, the senator from Oregon, who had been the running mate of John C. Breckinridge on the southern Democratic ticket. Representatives of the South joined eagerly in branding Johnson, a slave owner, as a turncoat and traitor to his own people.

Jefferson Davis called Johnson a "southern traitor" but Simon Cameron of Pennsylvania called him "lion-hearted." He began to receive letters addressed to "the only Union senator from the South." He also received letters that threatened his life and the lives of his family back in Tennessee.

In Tennessee, opinion was sharply divided. Among the people of the mountain region, who had few slaves and small need for slavery, he was supported. In the west and central part of the state, his name was cursed and he was hanged in effigy. This was a fair picture of sentiment in the border state Johnson represented in the Senate.

The arguments about secession continued. Senator Seward, the New York Republican, made a speech on the subject, giving a northern view. More southerners spoke, more vituperation was offered. On January 21, 1861, Jeffer-

son Davis withdrew from the Senate, since his Mississippi
had declared herself no longer a part of the Union. Then the
parade of southern withdrawals began. There was no hope
now, and everyone knew it, but the torrents of words and
abuse continued to stream out across the Capitol. Early in
February, Johnson arose again and defended himself against
the taunts of retiring southern leaders. It was a defense, but
it was also another call to arms for the Union.

Abraham Lincoln arrived in Washington during the last
days of February, hopeful that somehow the the tide of
secession could be stopped. But before he got to the capital,
he learned that the Crittenden amendment was dead. This
was a peace resolution introduced, without Lincoln's consent, by Senator John J. Crittenden of Kentucky. It would
have recognized slavery in territories south of a line drawn
at 36° 30', which would have included the areas of Okla-
homa, New Mexico, and Arizona that we do not now consider part of the slave question.

When inaugurated on March 4th, President Lincoln was
conciliatory but firm towards the South. He declared that
he had no purpose whatsoever of interfering with slavery
in the states where it existed. He also declared that no state
could lawfully get out of the Union on its own action.
Southerners were warned. If they persisted in seceding, the
Union would bring them back by force.

But many southerners really were not warned. They were
hypnotized by their own leaders and their own emotions
into believing that the South was as strong or stronger than
the North. Any student of economics could have told them
quite the opposite, but southerners were not consulting dis-
passionate students of economics in the first few months of
1861. Nor did many southerners believe that, when it came
down to the actual decision, the North would fight to retain
the Union.

When Fort Sumter was fired on and President Lincoln ordered Union troops to protect the nation and its property, Andrew Johnson went home to Tennessee to work for the Union. No one knew exactly what position this border state would adopt in the coming battle. Johnson had spoken for the people of the eastern half of the state. But Governor Isham G. Harris indicated that the state would side with the Confederacy if he could control it. He made a military agreement with the Confederate government, called for a large state army, imposed new taxes, and wired Lincoln that the men raised in Tennessee were being brought together to defend the state and not to help the Union.

On the train, heading south and west, Senator Johnson was nearly lynched near Lynchburg, Virginia. Several members of a mob caught at his coattails, pushed their way into his coach, and one man tried to punch him in the nose.

Senator Wigfall of Texas was also riding on that train, on his way home to join the Confederacy. Senators Johnson and Wigfall had exchanged more than a few harsh words on the Senate floor in the few months just past, but at one stop Wigfall persuaded the crowd to let Johnson speak. Johnson came out onto the platform, and in the midst of a Virginia audience overwhelmingly in favor of the Confederacy, he spoke for the Union.

When he returned to Tennessee, Andrew Johnson stepped into danger. He could not go much farther west than Knoxville, for beyond that point Governor Harris had men who would place him under arrest. One day when he went to speak in Bristol, in his own district, a mob started for the meeting house, determined to lynch him. But as the train came into the station, a young Confederate officer, Captain A. G. Greenwood, appeared on the scene. He announced that he had orders from Jefferson Davis, jumped onto the train, and told the engineer to speed to Jonesboro where Johnson would be safe. Perhaps the story is apocryphal, but it shows, at least, the tensions of the day.

Senator Johnson did not collapse in the face of threats. He set his pugnacious chin, armed himself with a revolver, and sometimes spoke with it in plain sight. One time when a member of a mob tried to attack him, Andrew Johnson fired a shot at the man as his train sped away. On another occasion, it was said, his old Whig enemy, Parson Brownlow, sent his son to warn Johnson that an angry mob was ready to attack him at a certain point along the line.

Loyalty to the Union created a new set of alliances in Tennessee politics. Senator Johnson found himself forced to join forces with old enemies and to abandon old friends. His Democrats in the west and central portions of the state were in favor of secession. The Whigs and others were for union. So Johnson found himself on friendly terms for the first time in years with John Bell and the parson.

An election was to be held in June in the state of Tennessee to determine whether the people wanted to remain with the Union or to secede with the southern states. For several months before it, Andrew Johnson did little but speak at public gatherings in favor of union.

One day at Rogersville, in Hawkins County, Senator Johnson came to speak at the courthouse. The town and much of the surrounding area was favorable to the Union, but there was a pro-Confederate military organization called "the Hawkins Boys" which was working for the southern cause.

As Andrew Johnson was speaking, Captain Fulkerson of the Hawkins Boys marched into the courtroom at the head of a party of armed men. He pushed his way to the front and ordered Senator Johnson to stop speaking.

Johnson looked the captain in the eye, and raised his hand to secure the silence of the crowd.

"Captain Fulkerson," he said, "I have been a Democrat all my life and accustomed to the rule of the majority; if a majority of this crowd wants me to stop speaking I will stop, but if a majority wants me to continue I will speak on, regardless of you and your company."

He then asked those who wanted him to continue to move to the right side of the room, and those who wanted him to stop to move to the left. A majority moved to the right. Captain Fulkerson saw that many of these men were armed, so he turned about and led his band out of the courthouse.

When the election was held in June, Tennessee voted to secede from the Union—or the majority of the state did. But the voting was by region. In eastern Tennessee, the mountain men voted overwhelmingly to stick with the Union. Seeing such defiance of the majority, Governor Harris prepared for trouble with the eastern section of the state as he led his countrymen into the Confederacy. He ordered General Felix Zollicoffer to march into eastern Tennessee and subdue any attempts of the citizens to work for the Union. The mountain men then either rushed to join the Union armies, or ran off to the mountains to form guerilla bands. Some, of course, favored the Confederacy even in east Tennessee, but it was apparent that the loyalty of the section could not be counted on by the men in Nashville and Richmond. The First District of Tennessee, Andrew Johnson's home Congressional district, gave more men to the Union army than any Congressional district in any other state.

General Zollicoffer and his men came into eastern Tennessee with the anger that can only be exhibited in wars between neighbors and relatives. They laid waste to the villages and countryside, killing and maiming the men they found, and mistreating the women.

Parson Brownlow was imprisoned; so was Andrew's son-in-law, Judge Patterson. Dr. Charles Johnson, one of his sons, was recruiting in the hills for the Union army, and Tennessee soldiers were looking for him to hang him. Robert Johnson, a colonel in the Tennessee cavalry of the Union forces, raised his own regiment. Dan Stover, Andrew's other son-in-law, was leading Tennessee mountain boys in guerilla raids against Confederate railroads and bridges. Andrew Johnson, now described in Memphis as "late United States senator, etc.," was warned that if he did not leave Tennessee quickly, he would be arrested and killed. He set out for Kentucky, leaving his wife behind. With three loyal friends, he headed for Cumberland Gap. On the way they were fired on several times, but escaped. Senator Johnson, of a state that had declared itself for the Confederacy, made his way back to Washington.

In Greeneville, General Zollicoffer and his men continued the search for Andrew Johnson, although they did not harm his wife in their home. But they confiscated his property and money, and Eliza survived only through the help of her slaves, who soon became former slaves. Eventually the General became so annoyed that he ordered Mrs. Johnson to leave her home immediately or be arrested; she then made her way slowly to the Union lines.

On June 22, the New York *Herald* announced that Andrew Johnson, described by the newspaper as "that staunch and fearless United States Senator" had made his way unharmed to Cincinnati, Ohio. From there it was a safe rail journey to Washington. As soon as he reached the capital, Senator Johnson called on President Lincoln to report to him of the loyalty and suffering of the people of eastern Tennessee.

Lincoln listened carefully, and then planned a military operation to move Union troops into east Tennessee. General Buell was in charge of this operation in the beginning, and some skirmishes were fought in the winter of 1861-62, including a small but important campaign conducted by Colonel James A. Garfield, who was later to become a major general partly because of it.

In the United States Senate, Andrew Johnson offered a resolution to arm the loyal citizens of the southern states, and Congress approved a sum of two million dollars to be used for that purpose. Senator Johnson also offered a resolution which was to show his stand on the war, and later, on reconstruction.

"The present deplorable Civil War," it said, "has been forced upon the country by the dis-unionists of the southern states, now in revolt against the Constitutional government and in arms around the capital; in this national emergency Congress, banishing all feeling of mere passion or resentment, will recollect only its duty to the whole country; this was is not prosecuted upon our part in any spirit of oppression, nor for any purpose of conquest or subjugation, nor for the purpose of overthrowing or interfering with the rights or established institutions of those states, but to defend and maintain the supremacy of the Constitution and all laws made in the pursuance thereof, and to preserve the Union, with all the dignity, equality, and rights of the several states unimpaired, and as soon as these objects are accomplished the war ought to cease."

After considerable debate, in which other resolutions were offered, the Johnson resolution was adopted as the policy of Congress toward the war, by a vote of 35 to 5.

In the summer of 1861, another Tennessee man came to Washington. He was Horace Maynard, who had stood against a Confederate candidate for election to the House of Representatives from eastern Tennessee. It was a very odd election, for if the southern candidate had won, he would have gone to Richmond, the Confederate capital, to serve.

But since Maynard won, he set out for Washington. Another congressman, elected under similar circumstances, was captured on his way to Washington, but Maynard reached the city safely.

Maynard came to see Andrew Johnson when he arrived, and the two Tennessee legislators went to call on President Lincoln. Under the decision of Congress, both were eligible to serve and represent their state, because Congress held that Tennessee could not secede from the Union, and, therefore, any duly elected representatives from that state were legally installed.

The two Tennessee men asked Lincoln to send a Union army to east Tennessee to drive out the Confederates and protect the loyal Union supporters who were in the majority there. Lincoln so ordered, in a directive to the War Department, but General Buell, who was in charge in that portion of the west, did not act. Summer and fall drifted along without any action having been taken. A convention of loyal citizens was held at Knoxville that spring, and met again in Greeneville later. The plan of these citizens of Tennessee was to form a new state, covering the eastern half of the area, but Confederate troops were so strongly entrenched in the region that the convention adjourned. Its members, among whom were Johnson's two sons, decided that no further meetings could be called.

In January, 1862, General George H. Thomas met a Confederate force at Mill Springs and defeated it. General Zollicoffer was killed in the battle. A few weeks later, Nashville was captured by Union troops, although east Tennessee was still held by the Confederacy.

Part of Tennessee was for the Union, but the people of this region were not the Union sympathizers that Andrew Johnson and his mountaineers from eastern Tennessee were. Many of them waited for the Confederacy to recapture

Nashville, and the Confederates promised that they would come.

President Lincoln wanted to win the sympathy of Tennessee citizens as well as the territory for the Union. With this aim in mind, he called Andrew Johnson to the White House and asked him if he would go to Tennessee as military governor. Johnson would. He resigned his seat in the Senate, took the rank of brigadier general, and in March, 1862, set out for Nashville to establish a new government for his state.

When he arrived, the new military Governor took possession of the deserted State House, the same over which he had presided as civil governor years before. He spoke to the people that first night, and soon issued a public address in writing which invited all to return to loyalty to the Union, promising amnesty to any but "conscious leaders in treason." His effort was not very successful. Most leaders took the position that the Confederacy had only begun to fight and that Johnson was the traitor.

Andrew Johnson's position was difficult from the beginning. He called on the City Council of Nashville for a loyalty oath. They refused to sign, so he dismissed them and put Unionists in their place. He called on ministers in the community for loyalty. Six of them refused to take an oath, so he sent them to jail. He sent known secessionists out of the area with warnings that if they returned they would be treated as spies. He taxed rich secessionist landowners to support the poor families of Confederate soldiers.

These acts did not endear Andrew Johnson to the Confederate citizens of Tennessee. They were watched closely by Governor Harris and his Confederate state government in Memphis, where they had fled from Nashville. Still Andrew Johnson was committed to a policy of stern government. He closed down the *Nashville Times* for supporting the Confederacy. On hearing of mistreatment of Union sympathizers on the other side of the lines, he sent messengers into Confederate territory at their own expense to warn the Confederates of the hostages in Nashville. Among others mistreated, if largely by neglect, was his own family. It would hardly have been surprising if Andrew Johnson had turned into a radical of the harshest variety, considering what had happened to his wife, sons-in-law, daughters, and grandchildren. Eliza Johnson was turned out of her house in the autumn of 1862 and arrived in Nashville in October, suffering from tuberculosis. One grandchild also had tuberculosis, and so did Colonel Dan Stover, Johnson's son-in-law.

In 1862, it was not at all certain that Nashville could be held by the Union forces. Three times military men made the decision to evacuate the city and then reversed it. Johnson determined that he would not leave Nashville and that he would not be taken alive, so he had the Capitol fortified. It came to be called Fort Johnson, and here, in the cupola, he and his staff often slept. His indomitable will shamed the military men. He continued to work for the Union, although he could not move away from Nashville, or make a public appearance more than ten miles from any Union army establishment without running the danger of capture or assassination.

For three years Andrew Johnson fought the civil battle of Tennessee, trying to bring loyalty where there was no loyalty, and trying to make friends with men and women who preferred to be his enemies.

One day General Ebenezer Dumont, the Commander of military forces in Nashville, brought a twenty-year-old girl named Laura Carter into the governor's office. She had been arrested for spitting on Union officers from the porch of the St. Cloud Hotel. The General had brought her to the Governor because she was the daughter of the proprietor of the hotel where Governor Johnson was staying.

"When I told her that she ought to behave herself while you were a guest at her father's hotel, she defied you and said she would yet dance on your grave," the General added.

Andrew Johnson raised his head from the papers he was examining, and smiled.

"Oh, you mustn't mind these little rebels, General," he said. "There is no harm in Laura. Dance on my grave, will she? She will plant flowers instead! I'll take care of her. Let her go."

Andrew Johnson was also capable of humor on other occasions, such as the time when the wife of a prominent imprisoned secessionist asked for a pass to go to see him. Johnson gave her the pass, reluctantly. She was a huge woman, and she offended his appreciation of beauty in the opposite sex. "If her husband had any sense of gratitude," Johnson told his secretary, "he'd send me a letter of thanks for sending him to a northern prison."

In 1864, when Lincoln examined his political situation, he found that he was far weaker in support than he had been four years earlier. Indeed there was much talk to the effect that he could not possibly be reelected. He decided that he wanted Andrew Johnson on the ticket with him for several reasons. For one thing, to have a candidate from a seceded state, and a former Democrat if not one at that moment, was an indication that the war was national in character and above politics. This would help impress foreign nations, too, that the South was divided. It should prevent many foreigners from providing assistance to the Confederacy. The point that the Republicans had joined a Union party would be well made by the presence of Andrew Johnson's name on the ticket. The one problem that disturbed Lincoln was whether or not Johnson had been an overly harsh gov-

ernor of the defeated territory. He sent a military advisor
to Nashville, and this man convinced himself that Johnson
had not mistreated the people or abused his power. So at the
convention of the Union party in Baltimore Johnson's name
was brought up. He was supported then by Parson Brownlow, who had been released from prison and had come north
to work for the Union. On the first ballot, Johnson received
200 votes for vice-president, Hannibal Hamlin, the incumbent, received 150, and Daniel Dickinson received 61. But
before the result was announced all but twenty-six had
changed to Johnson, and he was nominated to run with
Abraham Lincoln.

7 | ☆

Mr. Vice-President, Mr. President

THE political vision of Abraham Lincoln "the rail-splitter," and Andrew Johnson "the tailor," gave an aspect to the campaign of 1864 that cartoonists and commentators could exploit. They showed "Abe" and "Andy" at work repairing the splits in the Union.

It was good propaganda for the Lincoln-Johnson ticket and truthful propaganda. If Andrew Johnson was more inclined to harshness when he considered the aristocrats of the South, and if he spoke of "punishment" more than Abraham Lincoln did, Lincoln had said why this was so. He once observed that no man in the Union had sacrificed more or put himself in greater jeopardy than Andrew Johnson, who returned to Tennessee to try to stop secession and then risked his life to try to bring Tennessee and its people back into the Union.

In Nashville and elsewhere in Tennessee, the campaign of 1864 was fought as much with fists and knives as with ballots. Radicals, who supported the Union ticket, broke up the meetings of Conservatives who supported the Democratic ticket of General George McClellan and George H. Pendleton. There were many who supported neither, but nursed the hopes for the return of the Confederacy in their hearts.

To such a mixed crowd Andrew Johnson addressed himself on the night of October 24th from the south entrance to the Tennessee Capitol. He had determined that Tennessee would not desert the Union party, and he had campaigned vigorously all during the fall. This meeting of October 24th was the culmination of a torchlight parade in his honor.

As Andrew Johnson surveyed the crowd—generally a friendly one—and considered the history of the past few years, his face tightened in bitterness. Guerillas still infested his own First Congressional District. The state had responded so badly to the emancipation program that Johnson had hesitated to take President Lincoln's advice and use Negro troops to help him defend and pacify the area. He considered the insults he had borne, the demands for his assassination, the snubs of the genteel people of the area.

"What crime have I committed to merit such treatment?" he asked. "Has not my life been devoted to uplifting my fellow man, and to improving the general average?"

Privately, he indicated to his sick wife that he was desperately unhappy. "My mind is tortured and my body exhausted," he said. "Sometimes I feel like giving all up in despair, but this will not do. We must hold out to the end; this rebellion is wrong and must be put down, cost what it may in life and treasure."

He did not know—no one knew—that the South was nearly crushed; that six months after the election the Confederacy would collapse; and that he, Andrew Johnson, would be faced with the titanic job of trying to restore union in fact as well as in name.

When the election was held, Johnson's work in Tennessee was justified. Lincoln and Johnson carried the state by a majority of 25,000 votes. They received all but 23 of the 234 electoral votes of the nation. And even better, from Johnson's point of view, at an election in February Tennessee ratified the action taken by an earlier constitutional convention, liberated the slaves of the state, and paved the way for readmission to the Union.

After the election, Andrew Johnson collapsed with a severe fever which might have been typhoid. He felt too ill to attend the Inauguration on March 4th, and indicated that he did not expect to be there. Lincoln replied that he hoped Johnson would be in Washington on March 4th, and so Johnson, still suffering from fever, appeared in Washington, drank Hannibal Hamlin's brandy on the way to the Capitol Building, and delivered the confused, thick-tongued address that was to cause him to be branded a drunkard.

Scarcely was the Inaugural Ceremony ended and the second Lincoln administration begun, when John Wilkes Booth put an end to an era of American history with his distorted mind and lethal gun.

The war was over that April as Lincoln died. The problem to be resolved was a new problem—treating with the defeated enemies who were cousins and thus could not be so easily forgiven as total strangers might have been.

Much was forgotten and forgiven in the first few months of Andrew Johnson's term as President. The Johnson family moved into the White House in August, 1865—Mrs. Johnson, Judge Patterson, now a senator from Tennessee, Martha and Mary, Colonel Robert Johnson, the President's surviving son, and the grandchildren. The family went frequently on outings to the home of Francis Blair, where the President had recuperated from his fever; to Rock Creek Park, and occasionally to Pierce's Mill. The children chased minnows and frogs in the creeks, while the President wandered through the woods in the sunshine and shadow.

No one could take exception to the President's dress. He wore a frock coat and a clean stiff collar every day, well-cut trousers and well-shined boots. Mrs. Johnson—Eliza—was ill with tuberculosis, and so Martha—Mrs. Patterson—assumed most of the house-keeping duties. Some of the snobs of Washington society laughed to learn that Mrs. Patterson bought two Jersey cows and thus supplied the family with its own milk and butter. The Johnsons did not care. "We are plain folk from Tennessee," said Mrs. Johnson one day to a reporter, "temporarily in a high place, and you must not expect too much of us in a society way."

They were plain and unpretentious, too. One day, when the President's carriage was returning from a drive in Rock Creek Park, a thunder shower struck Washington and a torrent of rain began to fall in the streets. As the coachman slowed down in the midst of the rain, President Johnson glanced outside and saw a poor, ragged woman, drenched to the skin, making her way along the street. She was carrying a small child in her arms.

President Johnson stopped the driver and had the poor ones bundled inside the carriage. Then he took them home before he returned to the White House.

To say they were plain people, however, was not to say that they were rude. President Johnson entertained visiting royalty and members of the departments of government and Congress. He gave a reception for Queen Emma of Hawaii, widow of King Kamehameha IV, on her way home from a trip around the world. He attended a reception given by General Grant. He held other formal parties, usually in the Blue Room, although he was not by nature a party-giving man.

Andrew Johnson had a severe sense of propriety about gift-giving and receiving. It was the custom then, as later, for those who wished to influence legislation or other acts of government, to give gifts to those they wanted to sway.

Once, a wealthy citizen of New York tried to give Andrew Johnson a coach and four horses, worth six thousand dollars.

He sent them back, because acceptance of such a gift did not fit in with his denunciations of "extravagance, profligacy, corruption, and improper appropriation of the people's money."

In spite of this personal austerity and his unquestioned honesty, President Johnson fell into serious trouble before the end of 1865, and in three years became a figure to be hated and ridiculed. There were two reasons for this change. One reason was noble, if misguided. It was the fear of certain extremist abolitionists in Congress that the old social and economic systems of the South were not being destroyed and that the Negroes were moving back into a peonage which was nearly the same as slavery. The second reason, far less lofty, lay deep in the political hopes and fears of the Republican Party.

Andrew Johnson was a life-long Democrat. During the war years it had beeen useful for the Republicans to bury their differences with War Democrats who supported the Union and form the Union Party. But the union thus formed in politics was only skin deep. With the war won, it took no time at all for the Republican political managers of the various states to begin putting their houses in order. The old system was to be returned. It might not have come, or not so quickly, had Abraham Lincoln lived, for Lincoln might have forced the maintenance of the Union Party and might thus have created different political divisions in the nation. But with Lincoln gone, it was easy for the radical Republicans to convince themselves that Andrew Johnson was, after all, first a southern Democrat and then a Union man.

The view that men took of President Johnson and his actions all too often mirrored their own political ambitions. Thus his friends could declare Andrew Johnson "loyal to the Republican Party," which was really not the case, and his enemies could say that "his face was set as flint" against the cause of the radicals. Salmon P. Chase, Lincoln's Secretary of the Treasury, who nursed Presidential ambitions for 1868, could see nothing but evil in the man who might choose to run and thwart those ambitions. Senator Charles Sumner, Senator Ben Wade, and Representative Thaddeus Stevens all had reasons of their own for wanting punishment of the South—Senator Sumner for personal reasons to avenge an insult; Senator Wade and Representative Stevens for political reasons, to maintain Republican power.

The Negro was the pawn, except in the minds of a handful of idealists who hoped that the Negro could be integrated into American society. There were really very few such; most of what passed for idealism was desire for personal or political gain or hatred of the South that arose out of the war itself. At Dartmouth College, for example, the Phi Beta Kappa society called for Negro suffrage. To help the Negro? Not exactly. "Shall the horrors of Salisbury and Andersonville prisons, the murdering of innocent prisoners be forgotten and forgiven to unrepentant or lip-serving lying rebels whose oath is as naught under compulsion." That was how Thad Stevens put it. Vengeance, he insisted, was to lie in the hands of the North. There was more emotion than thought given to the issue of Negro rights and southern punishment in 1865.

By December, just before Congress convened, Thaddeus Stevens knew what he planned to do. He would keep control of Congress and of the nation, in the hands of the Republican Party. On December 1st, Stevens attended a Republican Party secret meeting, or caucus, at which it was to be decided what would be done with the senators and representatives who came to Washington from the states that had joined the Confederacy. Stevens proposed that each house of Congress agree not to admit southern representatives until the other house had come to the same conclusion. It was a shrewd move, because he knew that he could control the House of Representatives but that many of the Republican members of the Senate would hesitate to go so far in breaching rules of good conduct and decency to maintain political power. B. Carroll Reece, in his biography of Andrew Johnson, says that Stevens hated the South because Confederate soldiers had raided his home town of Lancaster, Pennsylvania, and burned his iron foundry, and that he hated Andrew Johnson for interfering with his acceptance of what we now call "graft," but what was then accepted by some congressmen as a right that went with office. Perhaps this was so, but the issues were not so sharp or clear. There was, as there always is, a resentment in the North against the people who had caused so much misery and heartache to the whole land, so many needless deaths of young men in blue and gray, so much starvation and torture and sickness. After every war there are people among the victorious who wish to wreak vengeance on the vanquished, and there are those who see in their victory a way of changing a social system they detest. Both these elements were at work in the immediate postwar period; they combined with personal hope for gain, personal desire for vengeance, and personal failure in statesmanship.

In a way Andrew Johnson could have been the ideal President for a postwar period. As did few others, he understood the South, for he had spent all his life there. He was committed to the side of the common man, but he knew the best as well as the worst of the southern social system. But his leadership was to be denied and fought every step of the way by Congress.

On the night after the first secret caucus Thaddeus Stevens attended a regular Republican caucus, and without telling the others anything about the secret meeting of a handful of the most recalcitrant Republicans, he proposed the resolution about seating the southern members. No one paid enough attention to realize what he was doing.

On Monday, two days later, when Congress met, the galleries were filled with men and women who had come to see this symbolic reunion of the states. The southern members of Congress, like lost sheep, had found their way home again.

But when the roll was called, the clerk of the House omitted the names of the congressmen from the South. Horace Maynard, the Tennessee Unionist who had escaped Confederate guns and had seconded Andrew Johnson's nomination at the Union convention of 1864, was one of those omitted. He addressed the clerk and asked that his name be called. The clerk, acting on orders from Stevens, would not listen to him. The clerk asked when the matter of admitting southern members would be taken up.

"I will press the matter at the proper time," said Stevens.

Then Schuyler Colfax, Speaker of the House, let the world know what Congress intended. All the reconstruction work done under Lincoln and Johnson in Tennessee, Louisiana, and other states was to be discarded, and reconstruction would be carried out once again to the satisfaction of the radical majority of Congress.

Out of this was established a Joint Select Committee of Fifteen, representatives and senators who proposed to take into their own hands the administration of the territories of the South which had seceded from the Union. The Joint Select Committee was headed by Thaddeus Stevens.

The seceding states of the South had complied with President Johnson's demands for reconstruction. The South *was* rebuilt in less than a year in the image that Johnson wanted, and which he felt was Lincoln's wish, too. So the infamous period known as Black Reconstruction was first to be prefaced by tearing down the rebuilding that had been done.

Lincoln had fought part of this battle in the case of Louisiana and the Wade-Davis bill, which stated that a President had no authority to admit rebel states into the Union. He had won the battle, first by vetoing the Wade-Davis bill, and later when Henry Winer Davis, one of its authors, was defeated for reelection in 1864. He had refused to surrender the executive power over reconstruction to Congress.

Now Johnson took the same position. He realized, immediately, that the radicals were putting party and personal hate and gain above the national good. And the nation, outside the South, was willing that this be so. It was easy to rationalize the failure of Congress to seat the southern members. After all, who were they?—four Confederate generals, five Confederate colonels, six members of the cabinet of Jefferson Davis, and fifty-eight Confederate congressmen. These were the leaders of the Confederacy. These were the men that Andrew Johnson had declared to be criminals. Who could object to wrath on the part of mothers, orphans, and those whose friends had died on the fields of battle, wearing uniforms of blue?

In his message to Congress a few days later, Andrew Johnson did not promise full social and political freedom for the Negro. Wendell Phillips, the old abolitionist, stated that "slavery is being reestablished by Congress" and refused to go to Washington when invited there, because he did not want to breathe the same air as such men.

What was the situation in the South? It was anyone's guess. Carl Schurz, a Missouri Republican leader, went south to determine the feeling of southerners for President Johnson and said there was no loyalty anywhere. General Grant went south and reported that the majority of southerners accepted the situation as settled—no states would try to secede again. The situation was whatever one wanted to find. If one believed the war was fought to end slavery, as the abolitionists did, and that the black man should be equal to the white, then reconstruction was not begun. If one believed that the war had been fought to put an end to the contention, heard earlier both in North and South, that a state could refuse to accept federal laws or secede from the Union at will—then reconstruction was probably quite complete.

Andrew Johnson had accepted Abraham Lincoln's emancipation of the slaves, but Johnson had never lost any sleep over the condition of the Negroes in the South. "Damn the Negroes," he once said, when charged in Tennessee that he favored racial equality. "I am fighting those traitorous aristocrats, their masters." He was not opposed to slavery so much as to the autocratic society that the system of slavery upheld.

Still, with all the complications that might be imagined in treatment of the South, had it not been for a handful of stubborn, selfish men, the difficulties between Congress and Andrew Johnson might have been resolved. The President did not declare war on Congress. The radicals of Congress declared war on him. *The Nation,* a magazine of New York City, noted that "if the President were to commit tomorrow every mistake or sin which his enemies have feared, his plan of reconstruction would still remain the brightest example of humanity, self-restraint, and sagacity ever witnessed— something to which history offers no approach."

Granting only half that fulsome praise, President Johnson must be given credit for good will in his attempts at reconstruction. Congress cannot be given such credit. Had the Johnson-Lincoln reconstruction program been followed, there is no telling what would have happened to the Negro—whether his rate of achieving education, equal economic opportunity, and finally social equality would have been speeded. But as reconstruction was to proceed, the scars left on the southern whites would remain visible and livid for a hundred years, and the whites would keep the Negro ill-educated, ill-housed, without adequate employment or opportunity for a decent life. Whatever else may be said about the Black Reconstruction that was to follow Thaddeus Stevens' declaration of war on Andrew Johnson, it cannot be said that it achieved the ideals claimed for the harsh program by its proponents.

Undoubtedly the desire for vengeance played an important part in determining the way in which Congress undertook to rebuild the South. Nearly a century later, it would be very easy to say that vengeance is not a proper basis for government policy. But Andrew Johnson once cried for vengeance. He was a stern governor of Tennessee when he was imposing military rule on people who had been his neighbors. His mind was changed, after the war, by many visits from southerners, and because as a southerner himself he found it easier to forgive those he had always known than a stranger might have. But he had made strong and sometimes wild statements about the punishments that ought to be given southerners. When he changed his mind, he could not expect all those who had agreed with him to change their minds. As President, he was determined to carry out reconstruction in his own way, and he did not listen to the voices in Congress which could injure his cause. By the end of 1865, then, the atmosphere of mutual trust and cordiality, which had certainly existed before, was gone. The radicals of Congress did not trust Johnson at all, and he returned the insult. It was apparent that trying times were coming.

8 | ☆

The Reef of Reconstruction

PRESIDENT Johnson was not the only one to send emissaries to the southern states to see what approach these new governments were taking towards the Negro and old property rights. The radical leaders of Congress sent their own agents south, and when these men returned, they told stories that enraged the legislators. Specifically, the southern states had begun enactment of laws known in Washington as "Black Codes" which were designed to control the activities of the newly freed slaves.

The harshest of these Black Codes were adopted by the states of Louisiana and Mississippi. It was particularly infuriating to the radicals that Louisiana had adopted such a code, for that state had been undergoing reconstruction for several years, since Union control had been established over New Orleans in 1862.

The answer of the radicals in Congress was to pass a bill which would establish a Freedmen's Bureau as a federal agency to administer the abandoned lands of the South and the affairs of the former slaves. The strongest part of the bill was a section which called for trial by military court of any persons who deprived a former slave of his civil rights.

The Freedmen's bill passed Congress in February, 1866. When it reached the desk of President Johnson he vetoed the measure, on the grounds that it violated the Constitution. First, said the President, Congress had no power to pass laws for all the states with eleven states not represented in Congress. Second, the provision for military trial was unconstitutional because it denied citizens the right to civil trial.

The President's veto reached Congress on February 19th, and the Senate at first refused to override it. It seemed to be a clear victory for the President, and a number of newspapers around the country supported his stand, calling Congress "a rump Congress." But Congress replied to the veto by a strong move of its own. House and Senate enacted a resolution against representation of any of the former rebel states until both houses should agree on admission of members. The interest of the nation quickened. What would President Johnson have to say to that?

On February 22nd, Washington's Birthday, President Johnson chose to make public his battle with the leaders of the radicals. Demonstrations in his honor were planned for various cities. In New York City, the Board of Aldermen endorsed the Presidential policy in a resolution. Elsewhere flags flew and cannons were fired in his honor, especially in southern cities where the people had become convinced that Andrew Johnson meant them well.

In Washington, a large crowd gathered outside the White House, demanding the appearance of the President. He came out to the terrace and spoke to the people. He referred to "the wicked rebel" who had been put down by the strong arm of government, but also to "another rebellion" aimed at overthrowing the Constitution and changing the American form of government. He said he had opposed secession in 1861, and that the secession problem had been solved, but that now, in 1866, other men were trying to destroy the Union in another way.

"Name three of the men to whom you allude," came a voice from the gathering around the White House.

"I say Thad Stevens of Pennsylvania; I say Charles Sumner of Massachusetts; and I say Wendell Phillips of Massachusetts," the President replied.

The next day, as the reports of the President's speech spread around the nation, they caused rejoicing in the South and among those in the North who were sympathetic to the southern cause. In New England, Ohio, and other areas where the radicals were strong, the President's words caused outbursts of anger. Uncommitted newspapers praised the President for his open stand. But in the end the brave words spoken from the White House terrace hurt President Johnson badly. For in them he had named names and had declared open enmity against three of the most important men in Congress, all of them men dedicated to radical reform. If there had been any chance of seeking a meeting of minds between President Johnson and his Congressional critics, this impromptu speech put an end to it.

Congress moved rapidly to seize the initiative. A few weeks after Washington's Birthday, both houses passed a Civil Rights Bill which gave citizenship to the Negro and guaranteed the same civil liberties to all persons born in the United States except Indians. Andrew Johnson vetoed the bill as unconstitutional and an invasion of the rights of the states. Congress promptly passed the bill over his veto.

At the end of April, Thaddeus Stevens and the other members of the Joint Congressional Committee of Fifteen were ready to report the Fourteenth Amendment to both houses of Congress. The amendment was the result of four months of Congressional hearings on the condition of the Negroes in the southern states. From studies of the results of those hearings, the members of Congress decided that the Negro needed specific guarantees of citizenship. They drew the Fourteenth Amendment to the United States Constitution in spite of the opposition of President Johnson. The law passed Congress in June and went on its way around the various states by three-quarters of which it must be ratified if it was to become law. Most of the southern states refused to consider the amendment because they claimed that it violated the rights of the states to govern themselves. From this came the demand that the southern states ratify the Fourteenth Amendment as a condition of restoration to full participation in the government of the Union.

At the end of the first six months of 1866, the original program of reconstruction was in shambles. There had been race riots in Memphis and in other southern cities, and afterward Parson Brownlow, the old Whig opponent of Andrew Johnson, who was now governor of Tennessee, had forced through the ratification of the Fourteenth Amendment. Tennessee thus became the first southern state to be readmitted to full equality.

As Tennessee was preparing this move, in Congress the Joint Committee of Fifteen reported that the southern states, by and large, were not repentant or ready to be readmitted to the Union's councils. The matter of reconstruction of this area, said the report, remained the responsibility and right of Congress and not of the executive department of government.

This odd interpretation of the Constitutional power of the legislative branch of government was passed over quickly by the radicals. Perhaps they knew they were on very thin ice, constitutionally speaking. It did not, however, deter them from taking the responsibility, because they had no further use for Andrew Johnson. They feared him too much as a man who would not counsel with them before taking action. In his message to Congress announcing the Tennessee ratification of the Fourteenth Amendment, the Governor of Tennessee referred slightingly to the President, and as they read the slighting statements, the radicals in Congress laughed.

Even as this occurred, President Johnson was making plans to take his case to the people. This had been his procedure in the days when he had served Tennessee in the United States Senate and the House of Representatives. In local political battles, too, Andrew Johnson had always found that if he could reach the people, he could make his case without the interference of interpretations from friends or foes.

Two plans were set forth. First the President's managers would attend a mass convention of the Union Party in Philadelphia on August 14th. Then Johnson himself would set out on a tour of the nation—"a swing around the circle" he called it, taking a term from the old days of Tennessee politics. Two points were to be resolved, although in his mind they were one and the same: his failure to endorse the Fourteenth Amendment and his veto of the Civil Rights Bill. His objections were on constitutional grounds, but his enemies made it seem that they were based on a desire to deal softly with the South for the sake of preserving the old southern ways. The President hoped that by talking directly with the people, he could make them see the issues in reconstruction as he saw them.

The convention at Philadelphia was an attempt to form a new party of moderates, who would oppose the stringent ideas of the radicals and "bind up the nation's wounds" with as little hurt as possible. Johnson and his supporters hoped to unite there the conservatives from the ranks of the Republican Party, who had no taste for the strong medicines prescribed by the radicals, with the old Whigs who had nowhere to go, and the loyal Democrats who had supported the Union through the war. The new group was to be called the National Union Party.

Political preparations began early, in Washington and elsewhere. Two delegates from every Congressional district, North and South, and four delegates at large from each state were selected to attend the convention. A special temporary convention hall, called a Wigwam in the fashion of the time, was erected on Girard avenue. Its builders boasted that it would seat 10,000 people.

The convention seemed to be called under the most respectable of auspices. General John Dix, Secretary of War in 1861, when the Civil War began, was temporary chairman. He was the man who had issued the order to shoot the first man who moved to pull down the United States flag at Fort Sumter, after the Confederates had fired on the fort and demanded its surrender. In the convention hall hung the United States flag and the flags of all thirty-six of the states that had constituted the Union, including those of southern states not yet readmitted. The note of this convention was that all should be returned to the Union as quickly as possible.

But the note fell flat. It was apparent that all was not right even from the beginning. East Tennessee, the independent, anti-slavery mountain area from which Andrew Johnson came and where he maintained his home, refused to send delegates to the convention in Philadelphia.

When the convention opened, and the band played "Rally 'Round the Flag," "The Star Spangled Banner," and "Dixie," and it was announced that delegates from Massachusetts and South Carolina were entering the hall arm-in-arm, the crowd began to cheer. General Dix announced that the southern states had accepted the conditions of showing allegiance to the Union, as demanded by the President, and thus could participate in this convention. The demands made by the Congress, he said, were subversive and dangerous.

It sounded wonderful and it looked wonderful to those who sat inside the hall. But from the outside it looked quite different. Many of the delegates were former southern leaders. Others, from the North, were men who had reputations as "Copperheads" during the Civil War. The convention was almost all "Copperheads" and former rebels, Horace Greeley wrote in the pages of the New York *Tribune*. The *Tribune* was a Republican newspaper, so Johnson and his managers paid little attention to the remarks. But the nation heeded them, in spite of the attendance at the meeting of Henry J. Raymond of the New York *Times*.

Since 1866 was not a Presidential election year, there was no national business to conduct save to establish a party framework and platform, and this was done. A committee visited President Johnson in Washington to assure him that the party was formed in unanimity. In accepting their pledges of loyalty and replying to Congressional critics, who now charged Johnson with wanting "dictatorial" powers, the President replied that if he had wanted such power, the way to have obtained it was to support the Freedmen's Bureau bill and seize the power through the opportunity there offered.

There was much logic in this statement, but there were other factors working in the nation, and they worked against Andrew Johnson.

Any and all violence in the South—and there was a considerable amount of it—was laid at the feet of Andrew Johnson and his "soft" policy. Before the National Union convention in Philadelphia, during the state convention in New Orleans to pick delegates, a race riot broke out in the city and forty people were killed. The radicals said the

Johnson men were to blame. How could they prove they were not to blame? In the difficult period of adjustment of the two races, there were bound to be acts of violence, fomented by both sides. But to the radicals, and increasingly to most northerners, the violence came as a result of southern whites attacking the defenseless Negroes.

"King Andy," they began to call him and the popular political cartoonists of the day pictured him in purple and velvet with a sceptre in his hand.

In July, three members of Andrew Johnson's cabinet resigned because they were not willing to oppose the radicals of Congress. The new men appointed were Republicans, not Democrats, but they were not radical Republicans. The schism had gone too far for such a course even to be considered.

On August 28th Andrew Johnson himself set out to undertake the second part of his campaign for victory and possible reelection in the fall of 1868. This was his "swing around the circle" to take the case for mild reconstruction to the people. It began with a trip to Chicago, where he was to address the Douglas Memorial Association, honoring Stephan A. Douglas, who had given his life to try to keep Illinois calm during the secession activity at the beginning of the war.

The special train carrying the Presidential party stopped first in Baltimore where 100,000 people turned out to watch the President ride by in a special carriage on his way to Fort McHenry. General Grant and Admiral Farragut, heroes of the war, were introduced and cheered. But, of course, Baltimore was a city of divided emotions, southern in its orientation.

When the party reached Philadelphia, the greeting was not nearly so frenzied. No Republican leaders showed up. In New York City, however, the bad impression of Philadelphia was quickly erased, as half a million people came out to see the party. But again, New York was cosmopolitan and Democratic in politics, and many of its leaders had done much business with the South in years past. The state legislature, meeting in Albany far from the big city, refused to pass a resolution welcoming the President of the United States to New York State.

Along the route from New York to Chicago, the train stopped often, and President Johnson spoke from the back platform. His message was nearly always the same in essence:

"I leave in your hands the Constitution and the Union," he told the people, "and the glorious flag of your country, not with twenty-five, but with thirty-six stars."

Everywhere his plea was designed to elect moderates to Congress in the autumn of 1866, and he called for the defeat of the radicals who would wreck his policy towards the nation.

By the time the Presidential party had reached Chicago and Andrew Johnson had delivered the Douglas Memorial Association address, his opponents had organized themselves to deal with him on the way home.

They planted hecklers in his crowds. They taunted him in the press. They insulted him and reviled his name. And Andrew Johnson replied in kind, in a manner quite fitting for a backwoods campaign in eastern Tennessee, but not one that the citizens of the nation were used to seeing and hearing from the Chief Executive.

President Johnson's friends warned him:

"Do not allow yourself to be drawn into extemporaneous speeches in the excitement of the moment," said Senator Doolittle of Wisconsin. "Enemies have never been able to get any advantage from anything you ever wrote," he said later. "But what you have said extemporaneously has given them a handle to use against you."

It was ever thus with Andrew Johnson, beginning with his badly timed, badly phrased, badly handled inauguration speech as Vice-President of the United States.

The tragedy of the trip began at Cleveland. When the party arrived at the hotel, a large crowd had arrived and demanded that the President show himself. When he appeared on a balcony, hecklers in the crowd began to shout:

"Hang Jeff Davis," said one.

"Hang Thad Stevens," said another.

The President of the United States then let fire, in his best Tennessee mountain fashion, and vituperated against the crowd and against his enemies. The crowd dispersed, taking away the hurt dislike of people who have been insulted by a politician. Only later did the Johnson men discover that it had been a put-up job, arranged by the radicals in Washington who had sent men and money. It had been the same in Chicago, except at the Douglas meeting. At St. Louis, the President was again trapped into making a loud, and unfortunate speech. The newspapermen with the party, most of whom were unfriendly, began to make innuendos which indicated that the entire Presidential party was on an extended drunken orgy. It was easy to believe this, reading of the excesses of language used by the angry President in replying to his enemies, and the Republicans in the North chose to believe that the President had become a sot.

It was on this trip, observing how the crowds reacted to his own appearances on the platform and on the back stage of the train, that General U. S. Grant began to have stirrings of political ambition for himself. But these were not very noticeable, and did not in any way change the results of the trip west.

In nearly every town and city there were incidents; heads were broken and people were killed. Yet because the Presidential party did not see many of these incidents, the group went on believing that the overall impression created by the tour was satisfactory.

Back to New York and Baltimore the party came, and on September 15th it arrived in Washington where manners were better. A large crowd turned out cheering the President and following him from the station to the White House, then demanding, in a friendly way, that he show himself once again before saying goodnight. This last friendly reception did much to wipe out the recollection of unpleasant incidents, and so Andrew Johnson was not alone in his belief that the tour had been a happy one for his political fortunes.

Gideon Welles, the Secretary of the Navy and Johnson's supporter, summed it up. "The President spoke freely," he said. "He wished to address the people face to face, a method with which he had been familiar in Tennessee and the Southwest. . . . When he stated the true issues to the people, they were obviously with him."

So Welles and the other Johnson supporters, themselves lulled, helped lull President Johnson into a sense of security—a feeling that he had bettered his own political situation and the program he favored by taking the case to the people.

It was not so. The horde of unfriendly newspaper writers who had accompanied the President saw to that. Perhaps President Johnson did appeal to the crowds where he spoke, except when he was heckled. But the reports of his speeches made the kind of reading that delighted the public.

Every excess or exaggeration was noted or multiplied. Words that in Tennessee would appear perfectly normal, caused Massachusetts citizens to shudder in revulsion. Important space was given to the replies of radicals whenever the President's words were reported. The charge was made again that the President was drunk—particularly at Cleveland when he was aroused to use such abusive language in answering his hecklers. And it made no difference that the charge was untrue. It was believed in enough places to send the President's stock tumbling.

In September, long after the trip was over, the echoes of it lingered on in the newspapers. There was one major issue in the elections to Congress in the northern states in the fall of 1866, and it transcended local issues far more than could be said of most Congressional campaigns. It was the issue of radical reconstruction versus the program of the President. There was, of course, another hidden issue, which a number of Presidents have ignored to their sorrow: the issue of local rule and Presidential pressure. No local party or local group of citizens likes to be told how to vote by the President of the United States. The radical press, shrewdly sensing this chink in the armor of President Johnson, made as much of it as possible. Wherever cartoons of Johnson appeared, they showed him in royal regalia, talking about "my policy." The words I and MY were repeated over and over. The implication was clear: Andrew Johnson was attempting to dictate to the people of the United States.

Andrew Johnson did not understand the image he had created, even if he could have done anything about it, which was doubtful, and so he persisted in the same way until the very end of the campaign. The result was all the radicals could have hoped for. The figures for the Fortieth Congress seemed nearly the same as those for the Thirty-ninth. In the Thirty-ninth Congress there were 42 Union Senators and 10 Democrats. In the House there were 149 Union members and 42 Democrats. In the Fortieth Congress, elected at the polls in the fall of 1866, there were 42 Republicans and 11 Democrats in the Senate and 143 Republicans and 49 Democrats in the House. But what a difference!

Nearly all the Republicans in the Fortieth Congress were radical Republicans, not conservatives. Andrew Johnson had set out on his trip around the country to save the Lincoln-Johnson reconstruction idea, and he had run the ship of state squarely onto a reef.

9 | ☆

Black Reconstruction

WHEN Congress met in December 1866, following the victory of the radicals at the polls, the Joint Committee of Fifteen was firmly in control and was determined that the treatment of the erring southern states should be established by Congressional will and not by that of the administration.

At the beginning of the session, President Andrew Johnson sent a restrained message to Congress, noting that reconstruction had been accomplished and that all that remained was for the Congress to readmit "loyal senators and representatives from the South." To fail to admit those representatives, the President said, would be unconstitutional, and a violation of one of the great principles of the Declaration of Independence: There shall be no taxation without representation.

The President was interested in preserving the letter and spirit of the Constitution, but the radicals of Congress were not concerned with the Constitution. They were determined to bring a social revolution to the southern states. Thaddeus Stevens lost no time in beginning. First he introduced a bill to abolish the state government of North Carolina and completely rebuild that state's structure.

In February, 1867, he reported from the Committee of

Fifteen a joint plan for general reconstruction of the South. The next month the plan was adopted by Congress.

It was quite unusual for Congress to be at work in Washington in the month of March. The workings of the government at that time called for regular Congressional sessions to begin in December and end in the first few days of March. The Congress that assembled in Washington on the first of December, 1866, was the Thirty-ninth Congress. Some of those members had been defeated at the polls, yet they came to Washington to make the nation's laws between December and March, as provided by the law. Normally, the Fortieth Congress, elected in November, 1866, would not meet until December, 1867. But this year the radical leaders of Congress were determined that they must run the government, and if they were to do so, they must remain in Washington and in session. So Thaddeus Stevens and the other leaders of the radicals pushed through a measure which brought the Fortieth Congress into session immediately on the heels of the Thirty-ninth Congress. On March 4, 1867, the Fortieth Congress began its deliberations, and so heavily was it weighted for the radicals, that there was no trouble at all in bringing about the program Thaddeus Stevens and the Committee of Fifteen wanted.

The Stevens bill for general reconstruction wiped out all the state governments of the South and substituted for them five military districts, each to be ruled by a general of the army. The entire South was to be placed under military rule (with the exception of Tennessee, which had already been readmitted as a state). There would be no rights of citizenship. The people of the South were to be treated as a conquered race, and they were to be ruled by soldiers under martial law.

Had this been the original program of reconstruction, conceived in the heat of the war, it would have been more understandable. Even southerners might have accepted, or at least bowed down to it as one of the inevitable prices of defeat. But it did not come immediately after the war. It came two years afterwards, when the South had been led to believe that it would be treated with humanity, when southerners had been allowed to go to the polls and vote for representatives and the southern legislatures had selected United States senators. In the South, the announcement of the terms of the Stevens bill brought fear and resentment. Congress was proving that those who fled to Mexico and other lands at the end of the war had not been misled in their distrust of the cousin-enemy. The worst feature of the Stevens bill, the proof that it was conceived in hate and bad faith, was the lack of a time limit. As far as Thaddeus Stevens was concerned, the South would remain under military rule indefinitely.

Fortunately Stevens did not rule Congress with an iron hand, although he could control it in all but his most extreme schemes. James G. Blaine offered an amendment which gave the southern areas at least a chance to escape from military rule. Any state which would adopt the Fourteenth Amendment to the Constitution and would change its state laws to admit Negroes to the polls on the same basis as whites, could then return to the Union fold.

This amendment to the Stevens bill was totally unacceptable to the southern states, but at least it offered them some escape from treatment as conquered territory, where Stevens had offered none. Stevens did not like the meddling with his bill, and he and his followers in the House defeated the Blaine amendment and passed the original bill. But Stevens could not control the United States Senate as he did the House of Representatives, and there the Stevens bill bogged down. The Blaine amendment was offered and the debate began. In the course of the debate the whole subject of

Presidential reconstruction was discussed, but the minority of senators who favored this method of bringing the South back into the Union had no chance of imposing its will on the large majority who insisted on retribution. Yet the minority had enough influence that the Blaine amendment was considered, and Senator Sherman of Ohio, brother of the famous general, was able to prepare a substitute. The reconstruction bill, thus amended, was passed, and Stevens, seeing that he could not have his way entirely, allowed the amended measure to pass the House, too.

Once the bill was accepted by both House and Senate, it went to President Johnson, who promptly vetoed the measure. Congress then passed the bill over his veto and it became law.

Under the new law the southern states were to call constitutional conventions to which delegates were to be elected by blacks and whites alike. These conventions were to establish state governments that would guarantee the Negro's political freedom.

Another law was passed at that same time to help Congress keep control of the reconstruction program. It was the Tenure of Office Act, which forbade the President to remove officers named by him with the Senate's advice, without the Senate's consent. It was vetoed, and passed over President Johnson's veto on the same day as the reconstruction act.

Johnson's vetoes of these two laws were hailed nearly half a century later as "masterpieces of political logic, constitutional interpretation, and official style." But on the floor of the House and Senate no radical leaders listened to the President's words or read them. They were not interested in law or logic, but in punishment and something else. Thaddeus Stevens was quite open about it now: he said his reconstruction program would assure the ascendancy of the Republican party for as long as he could foresee.

At this time Thaddeus Stevens was already talking about impeachment of President Johnson. He was talking of many things, this wild old man who hated the South and loved the Republican Party. One day he gave an interview to a reporter for the New York *Herald* which showed just how matters stood in the United States. Thaddeus Stevens did not know at the time that a stenographer was present at the interview and took down his exact words. Since the reporter did not seem to be taking notes, Stevens was quite open in his discussion.

He complained that the reconstruction bill had been "botched" by "demoralized Republicans" and he attacked Senator Sherman as "meddlesome."

He said Congress alone had the right to interpret the reconstruction law, and that the southerners, "conquered people," had no right to appeal to the courts to test the constitutionality of the law.

He said he would propose the impeachment of President Johnson as a matter of "duty and conscience." No evidence of treason or unfaithfulness to his post was needed. The President's official acts were enough.

He advocated the confiscation of the property of southern leaders and those who had been active in the Confederate fight against the Union.

He had no objection to bloodletting and violence if it were to be indicated in the dealings with the conquered whites of the South.

That spring of 1867, Stevens was riding high. When the South failed to call the conventions necessary to ratify the Fourteenth Amendment, Congress passed the first supplemental reconstruction law, which required the military commanders of the five districts to enroll voters. Not long afterward, the commanders were given further power over voters and officeholders. Finally came a measure that de-

clared that a majority of votes cast was sufficient to put a new
state constitution into effect, regardless of the number of
voters participating in the election. This last measure became necessary as reconstruction proceeded, and in several
states the white voters simply refused to go to the polls,
leaving the elections to Carpetbaggers—opportunists from
the North who went scurrying into the southern states to
make what advantage they could of the South's disorder—
and the Scalawags, the southern whites who, for reasons of
their own, cooperated with the military authorities and the
northern reconstructors.

President Johnson had no use for these laws. He believed
they had destroyed the Constitution. Thaddeus Stevens
agreed with him in part—he said that Congress had put the
Constitution aside for the time being. Whatever the way
of putting it, there is no question about the result. For ten
years, between 1867 and 1877, the United States was not
governed by its own basic laws, and the results proved that
when men, and not law, govern the affairs of other men, the
result is bound to be tragedy, disunity, corruption, and
tyranny. For ten years the South struggled under conditions
that would have seemed unbelievable to any Americans
prior to 1860.

There was much talk about a revolution in the South, but
it did not materialize. What did occur was the temporary
disfranchisement and misery of the white southerners, so
pronounced that when it ended, steps were taken to push the
Negro back, and consequently the Negro ended the decade
in no better condition than he had begun it.

Under the Presidential reconstruction, some states had
begun to treat the Negro as a human being. An Alabama
editor, coming to plead with Thaddeus Stevens, said that
his state was willing to give the Negroes the vote, to provide
for their education, to guarantee their protection in courts

and in society, and to send men to Congress who were loyal citizens of the United States. Thaddeus Stevens was not interested and would not listen.

One of the basic reasons that Andrew Johnson opposed the Congressional plans for reconstruction was his belief that the nation had prospered under the old Constitution. To enforce that Constitution, he said, there must be an intelligent and honest group of voters.

"Are the four millions of black persons who yesterday were held in slavery that had existed for generations sufficiently intelligent to cast a ballot?" he asked. He noted that intelligent foreigners who came to the country were required to remain in the United States for five years and show good moral character before they were admitted to citizenship.

"To give the ballot indiscriminately to a new class wholly unprepared by previous habits and opportunities to perform the trust which it demands is to degrade it and finally to destroy its power, for it may be safely assumed that no political truth is better established than that such indiscriminate and all-embracing extension of popular suffrage must end at last in its destruction."

These were wise words and they were borne out quickly. The Negroes were given the vote. Of course the majority of them could neither read nor write and knew nothing of politics except that the Union or Republican Party had set them free. They voted by symbols, and that is how the present symbols that characterize the political parties came into general use. Such symbols had been used before, of course, in the United States and elsewhere, but never had they assumed such importance as they did in the reconstruction period in the South.

One of the major forces in reconstruction was the organization of Union League Clubs, which sent Carpetbaggers into the South and published pamphlets designed to win the Negro vote for the Republican Party. Here is a portion of one such pamphlet:

Q. With what party should the colored man vote?

A. The Union Republican Party.

Q. What is the difference between Radicals and Republicans?

A. There is none.

Q. Is Mr. Sumner a Republican?

A. He is, and a Radical; so are Thad Stevens, Senator Wilson, Judge Kelley, General Butler, Speaker Colfax, Chief Justice Chase, and all other men who believe in giving colored men their rights.

Q. Why cannot colored men support the Democratic Party?

A. Because that party would disfranchise them, and if possible, return them to slavery and certainly keep them in an inferior position before the law.

Q. Would the Democrats take away all the Negro's rights?

A. They would.

Q. The colored men then should vote with the Republican or Radical Party?

A. They should and shun the Democratic Party as they would the overseer's lash and the auction block.

It was apparent that the radicals of Congress and their followers outside the Congress intended to create, if possible, a one-party state in America and to control it by controlling the Negro.

In spite of his questions about the constitutionality of the Congressional reconstruction program, President Johnson did his best to execute the laws passed by Congress. He appointed military men and sent 20,000 soldiers into the South. (They were joined there by Negro militia to help keep the peace.) The military governments took over the state office buildings. In all, 703,000 Negroes and 627,000 whites were given the right to vote, and in five of the southern states Negro voters were in the majority. The radicals had achieved what they wished.

Perhaps Andrew Johnson's position was impossible from the beginning. He had been, after all, a Democrat and a southern man before the war. During the war he had suffered and fought for the Union valorously, but when the war ended, and it became apparent that political control of the nation would be resumed, the Republicans wanted no part of the man who, quite accidentally and for political reasons, had been given the nomination as Vice-President of the United States.

In the first few months of 1866, the members of Johnson's cabinet who were loyal to him had begun to warn him about the danger of appointing so many radicals to high posts. Also, in his cabinet Johnson had retained Secretary of War Stanton, who was working hand in glove with the radicals and was their agent within the Johnson councils.

Johnson discovered the treachery of Secretary Stanton during the summer of 1867, in the trial of John Suratt, son of Mary Suratt who was one of those convicted and executed for the assassination of Abraham Lincoln. Mrs. Suratt had been convicted on scanty evidence, and the military court had issued a plea for mercy for her as a part of its findings. But when the plea for mercy reached the desk of Secretary Stanton, he removed it, and when it came time for the President to confirm the court's fiindings, and thus assure the execution of its verdict, the President did so without knowing all the facts.

When Andrew Johnson learned of this, he immediately demanded the resignation of Secretary Stanton. But in replacing Stanton he made another mistake—he appointed General Ulysses S. Grant to head the War Department, unmindful of the general's new political ambitions and the close relations between Grant and the radical leaders of Congress.

Under the Tenure of Office Act, there was some question as to the right of Johnson to remove anyone—including his own cabinet officials, and Stanton had the brass to question the removal when Congress resumed sessions four months later. Stanton later seized his old office and barricaded himself in there, and thus it remained while Andrew Johnson attempted to rule a nation whose political leaders seemed suddenly to have gone mad.

During the year 1867, six attempts were made to impeach Johnson, but all of them failed to win the necessary votes in Congress. Every possible manner of harassment was tried by the radicals, and it is safe to say that the American form of government was never in greater danger than between the years 1866 and 1868. In fact, the American form of government was quite suspended during this entire period, and instead of a Constitutional government, the people of the United States were shown an example of what could happen once the balance of power envisaged by the founding fathers broke down. The Presidency was rendered virtually impotent by a group of men in Congress who were determined to turn the government of the United States into a political machine. The man who tried, nearly single-handed, to stand against this onslaught was so roundly vilified and attacked that his name went down in history as that of an unworthy Chief Executive. But in 1867, when the struggle seemed at its height, it was not. The worst was yet to come.

10 ☆

Impeachment

FOR two solid years, beginning in 1866, Andrew Johnson and Congress had struggled, and with each skirmish fought in Washington, tempers grew shorter. Late in 1867, the southern states began to call the conventions required in the Reconstruction Act passed early that year, and early in 1868, new constitutions were emerging, directed by the radicals who had taken control of southern political affairs. Congress had, in effect, won the battle for control of reconstruction, but the contest had been so unpleasant that the radical leaders were not going to be satisfied with anything less than the disgrace of their enemy in the White House.

On one measure after another the procedure of passing laws had been the same. Congress passed a law; President Johnson vetoed it, giving his reasons. Congress ignored the reasons and passed the law again over the President's veto. By 1868, according to laws passed by Congress, the President could not appoint Supreme Court justices; he was forced to issue all orders to the military through the General of the Army under the Command of the Army Act; and he could not remove a cabinet official who turned against him, without the consent of the Senate.

After Secretary Stanton had resigned, and then reappeared and seized control of the War Department and barricaded himself in the office, the federal government threatened to break down. This was not the first struggle between the branches of government, and it was not to be the last. Abraham Lincoln had seized powers to which he was not entitled in 1861 when he called for 75,000 soldiers to protect government property in the South. In effect, he usurped the power of Congress to declare war in those first months of 1861. In 1867, the Supreme Court of the United States gave up its own power over federal policy when it refused to adjudge the constitutionality of the Congressional Reconstruction bills after southerners tried to bring these matters before the final court. The laws passed by Congress to control the actions of the Chief Executive in 1866 and 1867 would have destroyed the President's potency if they had been allowed to become the supreme law of the land. Andrew Johnson refused to accept these laws, and in so doing he laid himself open to charges of violation of the law.

It made no difference how ridiculous the actions of Congress might seem to the outside world in these postwar years, the radicals were determined to rule. Observers from other lands said the Constitution and orderly government in the United States were very much in danger in 1867, but Congress was too inflamed to take an objective look at its own actions. Some of them talked of abolishing the Supreme Court when it went against them. These same men sought to impeach President Andrew Johnson when he refused to accept the dictation of the oligarchy in control of Congress.

The first attempt to impeach President Johnson had come on December 17, 1866, when a congressman named James Ashley of Toledo, offered a resolution on the floor of the House. Ashley accused Johnson of many crimes, including participation in the assassination of President Lincoln. For two years Ashley was involved in various efforts to secure the impeachment. He and others searched the records of the trial of Lincoln's assassins for evidence to link Andrew Johnson with the affair. It was charged that they even attempted to buy perjured testimony. These efforts continued. No matter how many times Ashley and others were rebuffed, they still attempted to pin evidence of wrongdoing on the lapels of Andrew Johnson. They had no facts; they had nothing but personal privilege in Congress to make the wildest of charges. On a matter of personal privilege Congressman Ashley one day secured the floor and made so vituperative a speech against President Johnson that Speaker Schuyler Colfax, himself a radical and Johnson hater, felt it necessary to rebuke the Ohio man.

But the ridiculous affair of Secretary of War Stanton and his seizure of the War Department brought matters to a head. The radicals of Congress realized that they could not back down on the Stanton matter or their power over the Presidency would be lost. Nor did they want to back down. They had quite lost sight of the reason for federal government, which is to secure the best treatment of the people of the nation. They were goaded by their own visions of power, and they had forgotten right and wrong.

President Johnson, on February 21, 1868, told Secretary Stanton once again that he would have to give up the keys and get out of the War Department. Three days later, the Senate again denied the President's power to dismiss the Secretary of War, and the House on February 24th, adopted a measure calling for the impeachment of President Johnson. It was far from a unanimous vote: the tally was 126 for impeachment to 47 against. But the vote passed the measure. Every Republican voted Yea.

Eleven charges were drawn up against the President. The three major accusations said that he had violated the Tenure of Office Act by dismissing Secretary Stanton from office; that he had attempted to bring Congress into contempt by his speeches; and that he had opposed the execution of a number of acts of Congress.

In a case of impeachment of the President, the charges are brought by members of the House of Representatives, and they are heard by the United States Senate, sitting as a High Court of Impeachment presided over by the Chief Justice of the United States Supreme Court.

This trial was scheduled for high noon on March 5th, 1868, in the Senate Chamber. It did not actually begin until one o'clock because Chief Justice Salmon P. Chase did not arrive in the Chamber until that time. The Senators came forward, then, and took the oath which formed them into the Court of Impeachment.

So great was the public interest in this trial, that admission was allowed by ticket only. The galleries were crowded with diplomats, men and women with political influence, reporters, and the wives of senators and representatives.

"Hear ye! Hear ye! All persons are commanded to keep silence on pain of imprisonment while the Senate of the United States is sitting for the trial of the Articles of Impeachment against Andrew Johnson, President of the United States."

So began the Sergeant-at-Arms of the United States Senate.

After some preliminaries a summons was issued for Andrew Johnson to show cause on March 13th, why he should not be removed from office and perhaps even imprisoned. He could be tried by a jury, and if found guilty could be fined ten thousand dollars and imprisoned for five years for crimes against the American people.

The trial began on March 13th, with the managers of

House of Representatives in attendance and the lawyers for
the President sitting on the other side of the aisle from them.
Andrew Johnson, although called to attend his trial, did not.
He remained at the White House, attending to his job as
Chief Executive of the United States government.

The President's attorneys requested forty days in which
to prepare their answers to the charges, but the request was
denied. Representative Benjamin Butler, one of the impeachment managers, wanted immediate trial of the case.
Benjamin R. Curtis, one of the President's counsel, said it
was not proper to try to put through so important a matter
"with railroad speed."

"Sir, why not?" Butler demanded. "Railroads have af-
fected all other business, why not trials?"

The Senate, whose right it was to make the decision, said
that President Johnson could have ten days to answer the
charges. So the case was delayed until March 23rd.

Andrew Johnson worked late at night with his attorneys
to prepare the defense. Yet he could not give up his respon-
sibilities as Chief Executive, even as he worked and as he was
under fire from Congress.

And even as they tried to convict him of high crimes,
members of the House of Representatives were asking favors
of him, with strange results. A small island in the Caribbean,
called Alta Vela, had been seized by insurgents although it
was claimed by American citizens who had heavy invest-
ments in the island. One of Andrew Johnson's defense attorneys was an attorney for those who demanded action. He
asked that the President send a naval vessel to Alta Vela and
seize control of it for the government. The request was supported by Representatives Ben Butler, Thaddeus Stevens, J.
A. Bingham, and James G. Blaine, in spite of the fact that
the first three were managers of the impeachment proceed-

ings against Andrew Johnson. Johnson refused the request, a questionable one at best, and that particular defense attorney retired from the case.

The trial did not require many witnesses. There were twenty-five prosecution witnesses and sixteen defense witnesses. Not much testimony from outsiders was necessary, because the President was being tried on the basis of his official actions. Such matters as the charge that his "swing around the circle" was marked by much drunkenness would be aired—because the managers of impeachment were trying to destroy the President's good character. But the real questions were in his behaviour as Chief Executive.

On March 31st, all the written evidence was in the record of the trial. The first item was the President's oath of office, in which he had promised to support the Constitution. Another piece of evidence was the Tenure of Office Act. Another was his order removing Secretary Stanton from office.

As the prosecution made its case, it was apparent that the radicals in Congress believed they could run the impeachment trial just as they had begun to run the entire country's affairs. A witness said he was prepared to show certain facts. The managers of impeachment objected.

The evidence would be heard, Chief Justice Chase said. A radical senator objected that it was not for the Chief Justice to decide what should be heard, but the Senate. Chief Justice Chase ordered the Senate to come to order—and thus made it quite clear to all that the Senate was acting as a jury and not as prosecution, judge, and jury as some of the radicals wished.

On April 4th, the prosecutors had completed their case and it was left to the defense. On April 10th, the defense began its case. The lawyers called witnesses to show that the President had always acted in good faith under advice from his cabinet members. They also showed that during the

Stanton controversy, President Johnson had made efforts to take the question of the Tenure of Office Act before the courts for decision, but had been balked by the agents of the radicals in Congress who did not want the Supreme Court to rule on that particular law—so obviously improper was it for legislators to tell a Chief Executive that he could not pick his own advisors and department heads.

The trial of Andrew Johnson was marked by odd displays of emotion on the part of his enemies. One day one of the President's lawyers was taken ill, and a request was made that no further testimony be taken during that day.

Representative Benjamin Butler burst into anger.

"While these delays are taking place," he said, "and the Senate is being courteous to lawyers, the true Union men of the South are being murdered. On our hands and on our skirts is their blood."

His speech was the worst kind of demogoguery. Even his friends found it difficult to excuse, and it did untold harm to his future career.

As the trial closed, it was apparent that Chief Justice Chase had done his best to keep it from becoming a mockery. There was no justification for the impeachment in Constitutional law—it was the act of angry men who had been running roughshod over the laws for two years and who thought they alone constituted the highest authority of the land.

In the trial five of the conspiracy articles were shown to be ridiculous, and those charges were dropped. If there had been a conspiracy (as charged), then General Grant and other men whom the radicals did not want to attack would have been involved. But there was no conspiracy on the part of President Johnson to violate the laws of the United States, and it became apparent as the defense presented its case.

Others of the charges were also dropped. One charge was that the President had made a number of speeches using rough language and speaking in a loud voice. This, said the congressmen, tended to raise public contempt for the Congress. But when the charge was reduced to its real absurdity —that a President of the United States should be impeached for speaking loudly and roughly of a loud, rough, harsh body—it too had to be forgotten.

In the end, the case came down to one charge. Had the President of the United States acted improperly in removing from office the Secretary of War? Strangely enough Stanton, among all the cabinet officers was the one least likely to fit properly under the Tenure of Office Act for he had been appointed to office by Abraham Lincoln, not by Andrew Johnson.

At the end of the case Butler summed up for the managers of the impeachment. He indicated, as strongly as he could, that Andrew Johnson had been implicated in the murder of President Lincoln, although by this time nearly all the nation realized that the charge was foul. He called dramatically for the impeachment of the President. "The liberties, the welfare of all men hang trembling on the decision of this hour," he said.

Benjamin Curtis replied for the defense. He made a dignified reply, calling on the senators assembled to consult conscience and reason and not to be guided by party spirit, bias, or political scheming—as it was known so many of them already had been.

Looking at the case realistically, it is apparent that the Tenure of Office Act was passed not to protect any cabinet officers or any other government officials, but to hamper the President of the United States. Attorney Curtis made this quite plain. The other attorneys for the defense praised Andrew Johnson's patriotism and his conduct of his office and his love for the Constitution.

Johnson's enemies then had their opportunity to sum up.

One described the horrors that would befall America if Johnson was acquitted of these crimes. He said the President was no patriot. He charged that the President would drag the Senate behind him like a conquering Roman hero.

Thaddeus Stevens was a sick man at this time, and too sick to read his own address on the subject of Johnson's treason. He asked Butler to read it, and Butler did. "Any Senator who votes to acquit will be tortured on the gibbet of everlasting obloquy" said the manuscript of the shriveled little Stevens who nurtured so much acid hatred in his heart.

The impeachment trial was the scene of one of the most disgraceful exhibitions in the history of the United States Senate. Impeachment Manager J. A. Bingham spoke in favor of conviction.

"It only remains for me, sirs," he said, "to thank you, as I do, for the honor you have done me by your kind attention and to demand in the name of the House of Representatives and of the people of the United States judgment against the accused for high crimes and misdemeanors in office with which he stands impeached and of which before man and God he is guilty!"

Those words brought men and women in the galleries to their feet cheering, clapping hands and waving handkerchiefs. The people—as represented by this gallery—were calling for Andrew Johnson's blood. The Republican newspapers had done their job well, and the base emotions of the public had been aroused.

The Chief Justice shouted for order. There was no order. The crowd shouted and hissed. The galleries were cleared and the mob was actually driven from the Senate. Senator Cameron of Pennsylvania attempted to apologize to Chief Justice Chase for the disorder, but there could be no apology, and none was acceptable to the judge.

After this remarkable display of unfairness, the Senate

adjourned until May 11th, when the senators would meet
to vote on the charges.

The senators, of course, were supposed to vote their con-
sciences in this matter. But there was less conscience than
politicking involved on both sides. The Democrats and supporters of Andrew Johnson sought to persuade conservative
Republicans that there could be no danger in the acquittal.
The radicals sought to persuade the conservatives that there
would be every danger to the Republic.

There was more than vengeance at stake, too. Since there
was no Vice-President of the United States, Senator Ben
Wade, the President pro-tem of the Senate, would succeed
Andrew Johnson if he was ejected from the White House.
Such a situation would make Wade the leading candidate
for election in the Presidential campaign to come. And, of
course, Wade was a radical.

The radicals claimed to be confident of victory. "The
recreant will be out of the White House in a week," Representative Butler telegraphed the New Hampshire Republican convention that was meeting early in May. "Wade and
prosperity are sure to come with the apple blossoms."

May 16th was the date for the balloting. This time no
chances were taken that might lead to further disgraceful
scenes by the public. It was quite enough for the members of
the House of Representatives and Senate to declare their
emotions so forcefully; such declaration by the rabble was
not to be countenanced.

The galleries were crowded and the Senate was quiet as
the members of the House of Representatives filed into the
chamber to witness the voting. The radicals had one last
card to play. They asked that the voting on the articles be
taken, not in the numerical order, but beginning with
Article 11, the part of the impeachment charge that re-

ferred to the discharge of Secretary Stanton and the only part that still had a chance of standing up. The senators who supported Andrew Johnson objected, but they were overruled. The radicals feared that if the voting was carried in numerical order, the emotional result of all the findings of Not Guilty on the first ten charges might affect some of these senators, wavering on the legality of the final charge.

The radical idea was accepted by the Senate by a vote of 34 to 19, and the voting began.

Fifty-four Senators were to cast their votes, two-thirds of which were required to impeach the President. If thirty-six Senators voted to impeach, that was the end of the Johnson career.

A key figure in the voting was Senator Grimes of Michigan, who had wavered back and forth but had finally indicated that he would vote for acquittal. The voting proceeded slowly, until all the senators had voted. It began with Senator Anthony who voted guilty, and went as expected down the list until it reached Senator Fessenden, a member of the Republican Party. "Not Guilty" was his vote. There, the President had a chance. It proceeded until it reached Senator Grimes. He voted "Not Guilty"—another bit of help for Johnson's supporters. The radicals, who had been so confident of victory, suddenly were not so confident.

At the end the verdict stood 35 for impeachment and 19 for acquittal. The impeachment on the 11th charge, by far the strongest of the lot, had failed.

The radical leaders immediately began to charge that some senators had been corrupted. A committee was appointed to investigate.

The radicals did not give up quite then. The Senate was adjourned until May 26th, so that members could attend the Republican National Convention at Chicago. But that was not the only thought of the radical leaders. They hoped, at Chicago, to change enough minds so that Johnson might be convicted on one of the other counts.

But they changed no minds. On May 26th, votes were taken on the second and third Articles of Impeachment and the results were the same as on the eleventh Article. No other votes were called. The impeachment had failed and was at an end. Thaddeus Stevens was broken-hearted. He felt that revolution was threatening because a "peaceful" method of removing a President had failed. What Stevens did not seem to take into account was that an attempt by partisan political leaders had failed, not an attempt by the public.

11 ✰

The Election of 1868

On May 16th, when the first vote had been taken on the eleventh Article of the Impeachment charges and Andrew Johnson had been saved by a single ballot, Colonel William Crooks ran all the way from the Capitol to the White House to bring the news to the President.

Andrew Johnson was sitting in the White House library, talking to Secretary Welles and two others when the colonel staggered into the room, breathless and perspiring.

"Mr. President," he cried. "You are acquitted."

All in the room rose to extend their hands in congratulation, and Andrew Johnson accepted the gestures with warm response. Then tears began to roll down his face. He had stood fast during the anxious weeks, not showing how deeply this slur had hurt him. Now, in the moment of acquittal, those in the room understood the hell he had undergone, and they mused for a moment on the trials Andrew Johnson had accepted in behalf of his country.

It was only for a moment. Then the President rang for a servant and ordered whiskey, which the men drank in toast to the victory on Capitol Hill. In a few minutes others began to arrive from the Capitol to bring the news. The President remained with them for a little longer, and then moved quietly upstairs to visit Eliza, who lay ill in a room on the second floor of the Executive Mansion.

Six weeks later, when the Democratic Party convention opened in New York City, Andrew Johnson still had some hope that he might be nominated for a second term, although not by the coalition that had elected Abraham Lincoln and himself in 1864. The Union Party was no more. It was back to politics as usual, and the Republicans, in May, had nominated U. S. Grant for the Presidency. Andrew Johnson's hopes lay in the Democratic Party, where with General Winfield Scott Hancock and George Pendleton of Ohio, he was regarded as one of the prime candidates.

The first six ballots for the nomination were cast without any conclusive results—except to show that Andrew Johnson really had no chance. The Democrats did not dislike him—his supporters in Congress were Democrats and conservative Republicans. But the Democrats wanted victory, and they were quite certain that the nomination of Andrew Johnson would bring nothing but defeat.

Still, the Democratic convention declared its support of President Johnson and his policies. Francis P. Blair, one candidate before the convention, said that the President ought to refuse to enforce the radical reconstruction program of Congress. Johnson would not go so far. He was one of the few men elected by the American people in those years who believed in a strict construction of the American Constitution. He also believed that the nation was courting disaster in its acceptance of the Republican insistence that the Constitution be "suspended" until the Congress had finished what it set out to do.

The Democratic convention finally nominated Horatio Seymour, Governor of New York. In the campaign that followed, it was apparent that Thaddeus Stevens and the radicals in Congress had read the temper of the nation shrewdly, and that there was reason behind their insistence that the South be reorganized so that the Republicans could hold power there. In elections in 1867, the Democrats had won many posts in New England, the Middle Atlantic States, and the West. Boston, that year, elected a Democrat as mayor.

No wonder Thaddeus Stevens shook with rage when he considered Andrew Johnson and the plight of his Republican Party. No wonder the radicals in Congress forced through the reconstruction of Carpetbag and Scalawag. By election day, 1868, nine southern states had ratified the Fourteenth Amendment. All of them, of course, were safely under control of the radicals, who could manipulate the Negro vote. The Negro vote came to 700,000 ballots. In the election, the Republicans won by 300,000 votes. General Grant won electoral votes in all but eight states, so even if the Democrats had been in control of the South they probably would not have won the election of 1868. But there is no doubt that the Republican victory came from the use of Negro votes and what was called "waving the bloody shirt of the rebellion," or hammering the American voters with the responsibility of the Democratic South for the Civil War.

Once the election was over, Andrew Johnson could settle down to clearing up the loose ends of his administration, and preparing to return to Tennessee after March 4th, the day in 1869 when Ulysses S. Grant would become President of the United States. But there were still things to be done, and there was some pleasure in doing them. Secretary Stanton, who had brought about the impeachment, had resigned. He was ill and out of politics. Thaddeus Stevens, the most potent enemy Johnson ever faced, died in August before the election. Senator Ben Wade, another enemy, was defeated for reelection. Congressman Ashley, who had brought ridiculous charges, including that of Johnson's participation in the assassination of Lincoln, disappeared.

And when these men dropped out of the political scene, suddenly the pressures against Andrew Johnson decreased. When, on Christmas Day, 1868, the President declared a general amnesty for all who had served the Confederacy, even including Jefferson Davis, the nation cheered, and even the most radical of Republicans could do no more than gnash their teeth. The nation was growing tired of constant reminders that the wounds were not yet bound up.

Aside from the overriding issue of reconstruction, in which Andrew Johnson battled for moderation and lost to the revolutionaries in Congress, the Johnson years in the White House encompassed enough issues to make him remembered as a visionary and forthright President. Yet much of what he did has been forgotten or attributed to other men.

In 1863, when the United States was caught in the Civil War, Napoleon III, Emperor of France, decided to make Mexico a French colony. The brother of the Emperor of Austria, Maximilian, was sent to Mexico to rule. In 1865, when the Civil War was over, General Grant wanted to march into Mexico and go to war against the French. President Johnson prevented an open breach, because the Europeanized government of Mexico was falling anyway.

In foreign policy the most important accomplishment of the Johnson administration was the purchase of Alaska from Russia. Usually in history books credit for this action is given to Secretary of State Seward. That, again, is a matter of fashion in history. In some cases, where the President has been a popular man, he is given credit and blame for all that occurred in his administration. In others, where the President has been unpopular, newspapers and magazines and books of the period credit others, and this tends to keep on happening even a hundred years or more later. As much as Thomas Jefferson was responsible for the Louisiana Purchase from Napoleon I, Andrew Johnson was responsible for the purchase of Alaska. The Senate ratified the treaty, but the House, where Johnson was even more hated, refused to vote any money for it. "Johnson's polar bear garden" they called it, and cartoonists of the day showed King Andy in various unfavorable poses. Citizens of the state of Alaska in the Twentieth Century would be surprised to know that "the products of Alaska are polar bears and icebergs; the vegetation is mosses; the ground freezes there six feet deep; and the streams are glaciers."

Had it been left to Congress, Alaska would yet be Russian territory. The United States Supreme Court had held earlier that the Senate could not ratify a treaty that involved payment of federal funds without the consent of the House of Representatives. That was part of the Constitutional plan that the House of Representatives, as the most direct link with the people, should control financial affairs for the government. The House, under Thaddeus Stevens, could not be expected to favor anything the administration wanted. So there seemed every possibility that Alaska would be lost to the United States.

Russian-American relations, however, were very close in the 1860's. The Russians had been the only European friends of the Union during the Civil War. The French had used that struggle to establish an empire on the southern border of the United States. England had favored the South as much as was possible without actually declaring war on the Union. Spain, with colonial interests that confronted those of the United States, was also unfriendly to the Union. Russia, however, had supported the Union, and now she agreed to wait for the money on the purchase of Alaska. The next move was up to the President.

President Johnson did not wait for Congressional approval. In October, 1867, he took possession of Alaska and ordered the American flag flown over Sitka, as Russian and

American soldiers paraded. The changing of the colors was accomplished. Congress fumed and fussed, but finally in the summer of 1868, passed the bill appropriating the money for the Alaska purchase. Had President Johnson not acted, the British would have done all possible to secure Alaska and add it to their Canadian holdings.

Faced with huge federal indebtedness at the end of the Civil War, President Johnson handled fiscal affairs very badly, and if his policies did not cause the Panic of 1873, at least the concept of payment in Greenbacks, or paper money, instead of metal—and particularly gold—was one cause of the panic. President Johnson also established a precedent in international policy which was to live on and haunt Americans in a later period. The United States government owed a considerable sum of money to England and had issued bonds which bore interest at six percent to secure the loans. In 1868, Andrew Johnson suggested that the English ought to consider the six percent interest payments as principal payments. In that way the bonds could be retired in less than twenty years. What he was asking for was a reduction in the debt to England, no matter what he called it. England and other countries were to remember that, and after World War I, when they owed the United States a great deal of money, they followed the policy that Andrew Johnson had announced a half-century before.

President Johnson's relations with President-elect Grant were not what might have been expected. Grant had supported the Johnson policies and had assisted in making them from time to time, as when he traveled to the South to report on conditions there, and when he served briefly as head of the War Department. Perhaps it was the influence and pressures of the radicals which caused him to change. Perhaps, also, it was the feeling of guilt that a man has toward someone he has wronged. In any event, Grant grew frigid toward Andrew Johnson in the last days of the "Lame Duck" administration. Johnson appointed Grant's brother-in-law to an important post, but that did not help. Johnson invited Grant to the White House, but Grant would not come.

One interesting note about Andrew Johnson was that, while he was not a Roman Catholic, so great had been the excesses of the Protestant churches against him, and particularly of the Methodist group he favored, that the President began attending services at St. Patrick's Catholic Cathedral. In the end, he was to die and be buried without a religious ceremony, but he kept the kindest feeling toward Roman Catholicism, because in his hours of trial that church almost alone took no stand against him. Furthermore, he approved thoroughly of the Roman Catholic manner of treating rich and poor alike. He said exactly that.

After the two nominating conventions had picked their candidates, even while the Republicans continued to assassinate Andrew Johnson's character, the sentiment in the nation changed toward the President. From Boston, John Quincy Adams II wrote to the President, praising him for standing true to the Constitution at a time when others were ignoring it. Hundreds of people came to the Presidential receptions at the White House.

As the time for inauguration of the Grant administration came closer, this question was raised at the White House: Should the President attend the ceremony or should he stay away? There were precedents for attendance and precedents for absence. Some members of the cabinet wanted President Johnson to go, but Grant's refusal to attend the New Year's reception and others made it apparent that there would be no friendliness between the two. So Andrew Johnson decided to stay at the White House while his successor took the oath of office.

Rather, he decided to stay until Grant took the oath. In
the last few days before March 4th, the President's household was engaged in packing and sending possessions back
to Tennessee. There were not many possessions that the
Johnsons had not purchased for themselves. For at a time
when most men regarded public office as a place for the
acquisition of personal wealth, Andrew Johnson took the
opposite view. He refused, always, to accept valuable gifts,
although dozens of them were offered to him. In his term of
office, congressmen and senators were growing rich in the
taking of moneys that would now be considered as bribes.
To be sure, it was the custom. Public morality among the
majority of politicians was extremely low—so low that at
one time a few years later, Boss Tweed controlled the entire
legislature of New York through bribes. But not all sense of
public morality was low, and the most outstanding example
of high morality in public office was Andrew Johnson, whose
record would stand against that of any president who ever
occupied the White House.

On the morning of March 4th, all was packed, and
Andrew Johnson sat in his office signing bills and dictating
memoranda which would be given to Ulysses S. Grant for
whatever use he wished to make of them. Andrew Johnson
did not propose to see the new President at all.

As the clock struck noon and U. S. Grant made ready to
take the oath of office, Andrew Johnson left the White
House and drove to the house of an old friend, Johathan
Coyne, editor of the *Intelligencer*. Mrs. Johnson had left
the hubbub of the White House and gone there a few days
earlier.

The national capital was filled with the sounds of boom-
ing cannon, the marching of feet, and later in the day and
night, the laughter of women, and the deep voices of satisfied men who were celebrating the coming to office of the

Grant administration. Among them the spoilsmen led the merrymaking. They laughed louder and longer than any others. In the eight years to come, they were to carry on the most depraved and corrupt government in the history of the Union. Public office was to cease to be a public trust, and the public was almost to forget that others, like John Quincy Adams, had regarded government as a sacred trust. These men, then, were in no mood to read or pay attention to the final message of Andrew Johnson as he left the White House. It was an account, for the American people, of Johnson's stewardship of the Presidency. More, it was a report to Americans of what had been done to drag the nation down, and a warning for the future.

"The servants of the people in high place," the message said, "have betrayed their trusts for personal and party purposes. While public attention has been constantly turned to the past and expiated sins of the South, these servants . . . have broken their oaths of obedience to the Constitution and undermined the very foundations of liberty, justice, and good government. When the rebellion was being suppressed by the volunteered services of patriot soldiers amid the dangers of the battlefield, these men crept without questions into place and power in the national councils. After all danger had passed, when no armed force remained, when a punished and repentant people lowered their heads to the flag and renewed their allegiance to the government of the United States, then it was that these pretended patriots appeared before the nation and began to prate about the thousands of lives and millions of treasure sacrificed in the suppression of the Rebellion. They have since persistently sought to inflame the prejudices engendered between the sections, to retard the restoration of peace and harmony, and by every means to keep open and exposed to the poisonous breath of party passion, the terrible wounds of a four-year war. They have prevented the return of peace and the restoration of the Union and in every way, rendered delusive the purposes, promises, and pledges by which the army was marshalled, treason rebuked, and rebellion crushed, and made the liberties of the people and the rights and powers of the President objects of common attack. They have attempted to place the President under the power of a bold, defiant and treacherous cabinet officer. They have robbed the Executive of the prerogative of pardon, rendered null and void acts of clemency granted to thousands of persons under provisions of the Constitution, and committed gross usurpations by legislative attempts to exercise this power in favor of party adherents. They have conspired to change the system of our government by preferring charges against the President in the form of articles of impeachment, and contemplating, before hearing or trial, that he should be placed under arrest, held in durance, and, when it became their pleasure, to pronounce his sentence, driven from place and power in disgrace."

Thus did Andrew Johnson sum up his indictment of the Congress of the United States. Citizens in later years, able to view the period of 1865-1868 without the passions of contemporaries, would not have to agree with all that Johnson said to realize that the established form of government of the United States faltered in those years and was, in effect, suspended—at least as far as the citizens of the South were concerned.

It was apparent, too, that the one deterrent to the unruly, angry, and selfish men of the radical movement was the Constitution of the United States. These men said they would suspend the Constitution—and they did. They would gladly have destroyed it, but they feared the people too much. Two branches of government, the legislative and judicial, ignored the Constitution, the one in deliberate anger, the other in self-protection and fear. One branch, the executive, upheld it, cited it, and wrapped itself in the words of the document, never letting the people forget that the Constitution meant more than all presidents, congressmen, and judges combined, for through that document came the assurance of orderly transition of government and the only effective guarantees to the people that could be counted on to surmount the emotions of any and all times.

The guarantees, if invoked, would have saved the South from Black Reconstruction. The suspension of the Constitution allowed the social revolution that was started, but was not to be finished for more than a century.

Andrew Johnson was not concerned with the social revolution. He regarded himself, as President, as the steward of the people. When he stepped down from his high post in Washington, he did so with the warning to the people that they could not afford to allow men of little faith and much cupidity to direct and judge the people's affairs without the control of the nation's basic document.

Having said this much, Andrew Johnson was ready to go home.

12 ☆

Vindication of a President

WHAT was Andrew Johnson to do with himself when he vacated the Presidency? He was sixty-two years old and filled with anger against the men who had destroyed him politically.

Andrew Johnson's answer was to devote the rest of his life to vindication of his character. Those were his own words. His actions supported them.

On his return to Greeneville he found a banner stretched across the main street. "Welcome Home, Andrew Johnson, Patriot," it said. Eight years before, when he left his home in such a hurry to escape imprisonment by the Confederate government, a banner had also been stretched across the street. "Andrew Johnson, Traitor," it had read. Times had changed. The nation had undergone trial by fire. And while Andrew Johnson was now regarded by the radicals as a traitor, the men and women who knew him best knew also what he had sacrificed and what he had done for his country.

As he left Washington, the retiring President was deluged with invitations to visit various cities and even foreign lands, but he made only one trip, to Baltimore, where he was treated as a conquering hero.

Of course, it was a southern city. By honoring Andrew Johnson Southerners could also show their dislike of the

Republicans and radical reconstruction. But that was not the only reason. At Lynchburg, where he had been shot at one time and burned in effigy during the war, Andrew Johnson was greeted with honor. At Bristol, on the Tennessee border, a delegation from Greeneville met the train to accompany him home again.

Home again, and installed in the brick house he had not seen for so many years, Andrew Johnson took no time to relax. He began, immediately to campaign for his election by the state legislature as United States senator. The best way he could think of to vindicate himself as President was to return to Washington and fight in the very body that had attempted to destroy him—Congress.

This was no easy matter in reconstructed Tennessee. The state had been readmitted to the Union in July, 1866, when it accepted the Fourteenth Amendment to the Constitution, but affairs were in the hands of Carpetbaggers and Scalawags here as in other southern states. The governor of the state was Parson Brownlow, Andrew Johnson's sometimes friend and sometimes enemy. Brownlow was honest, although a radical. One could not say the same for the men who followed him. They were called "Black and Tan" by the outraged southerners, because most of these office holders were Negroes or mulattoes—the common term for those of mixed blood. Tennessee, the first state readmitted from the South, was also the birthplace of the Ku Klux Klan, the fraternal organization which became the terror of the Negroes in all the South. General Nathan B. Forrest, hero of the Confederate army, was the first Grand Wizard of the organization, and by the time Andrew Johnson returned to Tennessee there were hundreds of thousands of Klan members in the South. They were engaged in a reign of terror against the Negroes who held political power.

The state was as sharply divided as ever. Union supporters

ruled. Confederate supporters ruled at night and through hatred and fear. In the year that ended in June, 1868, one hundred and sixty-two people were murdered in Tennessee, most of them by the Klan and similar organizations. So great was the threat of the Klan to government that Governor Brownlow determined to suppress it. A special session of the legislature in 1868, passed severe laws against the Klan. Its members were declared to be outlaws and where found, they were to be punished with death.

The Republicans of Tennessee were divided among themselves, too. In May, 1869, the conservative Republicans nominated one candidate and the radicals, another. The issue was Negro domination of the state government which the conservatives no longer supported. Parson Brownlow, who had deserted the governor's chair to become United States senator, supported the conservative side.

That summer, after he returned home, Andrew Johnson stumped the state for the conservatives. It was a dangerous business, and he was often threatened by the crowds he spoke to, particularly the radicals, who seemed to have no end of hatred for him. He spoke anyhow. And when the election was held in August, 1869, the conservatives won control of the Tennessee legislature and the conservative candidate was elected governor by 50,000 votes.

Andrew Johnson hoped and expected that the conservative legislature would choose him as United States senator, but President Grant managed to secure his defeat by putting into the hands of Senator Brownlow, rather than Governor Senter, Johnson's man, the control of patronage in the state of Tennessee. A trusted friend of Johnson's, his former private secretary in fact, turned against him at a crucial moment, because the secretary's brother was promised the Senate seat. The deal was made, and Johnson was defeated by a very narrow margin in the legislature.

Three years later Andrew Johnson ran for the post of Congressman-at-large, but was again defeated. Johnson ran as an independent candidate, and he secured many Democratic votes but the Republicans, secure in the control of patronage in the state, held the party together and elected a Republican.

In this election, Andrew Johnson took a middle position which was so typical of him, and which was the reason for his many defeats as President in the years between 1865 and 1868. It is illustrated very well by the Johnson position on the Negro vote.

"The Radical Congress made a serious blunder when they enfranchised the Negro race as a whole, before they were qualified to vote," he said. "This matter should have been left to the individual states. But let bygones be bygones and let us live together in peace and good fellowship; after an honest trial, if it is found that we can't live in peace, let it be arranged, by voluntary colonization or otherwise, that we may part in peace."

At one political meeting in which there was a crowd of Negroes, Johnson addressed them directly.

"If fit and qualified by character," he said, "no one should deny you the ballot. I have been ridiculed for saying I will be your Moses, yet I say again, I will be your Moses; and if you have a certificate to vote you should be allowed to vote."

That day Andrew Johnson called an old colored man to him, and in his best oratorical manner, placed his hands on the man's white woolly head and blessed him, then told him to go out and labor for the good of his race.

This attitude was not one to endear Johnson either to the radicals, who found him intolerable, or to the former Confederates, who were frightened of miscegenation and Negro control of their lives.

But Andrew Johnson's persistent defense of his conduct

over the years finally brought him back to public life. On January 26, 1875, the Tennessee legislature was badly divided in its support of candidates for the United States Senate seat of Parson Brownlow. On the fifty-fifth ballot the post was won by Andrew Johnson. It was six years since he had been in the White House, and in the political events of those six years lay the reason for his return to political office.

Little by little, Andrew Johnson's policies were being vindicated in Washington. In 1869, Ulysses S. Grant discovered that the Tenure of Office Act made life intolerable for a President, and he sought its repeal. The House of Representatives passed such a measure, but the Senate refused to reverse itself. The struggle over appointments made thinking men wonder.

The first four years of Grant's administration were not ended when the public began to realize that Washington was a hotbed of corruption and scandal. Many of Grant's appointees were robbing the Treasury. Andrew Johnson said scornfully that offices were being sold to the highest bidders, and there seemed to be some truth in the charge. The Credit Mobilier scandal erupted, implicating many high officials, including Schuyler Colfax, Vice-President of the United States. Congressmen and senators who had been attacking Andrew Johnson as a traitor a few years before were now discovered to have been taking bribes at the very time they were attacking Johnson. So serious had the situation become by 1872, that the Republican Party split. The supporters of Grant ignored the wrongdoing. More conservative Republicans could not stomach it, and they deserted the fold to run Horace Greeley for President.

The election of Andrew Johnson to the Senate was brought about by a combination of Democrats and conservative Republicans. It was a narrow victory—won by a single vote, but it was victory and that was what counted.

Andrew Johnson was eager to return to Washington. He

had strong feelings about the conduct of the American government in the past six years. His self-appointed task in the Senate would be to publicize the wrongs of the Grant administration.

Andrew Johnson had $73,000 on deposit with the Washington branch of the Jay Cooke banking house when that famous firm collapsed in the Panic of 1873. The money represented almost his entire life savings. But as with thousands of other depositors, he was given no warning of the difficulties of the firm. He hurried to Washington in 1873, to discover what had happened and how he might recover something. He found that the Cooke banking house had been operating for months on government money—deposits made in the banks by the federal government, but used by the bankers as if it was their own money. The bank examiners, apparently, had been bribed. A large number of congressmen owed money to the Cooke banking house and were thus in no position to look into its affairs very carefully.

Apparently the Cookes had bought protection from audits for several years, but finally, their unwise investment in backing the Great Northern Railroad had ruined them, and the situation could not be concealed.

Andrew Johnson was most indignant because he learned that Henry Cooke had warned President Grant and other radical leaders who had deposits in the bank in time for them to save their money, but had allowed the general public to lose all. When he was in Washington investigating these matters, a crowd collected in front of the Metropolitan Hotel where he was staying and demanded his appearance and a speech. From the balcony of his hotel room Andrew Johnson did make a speech, castigating the administration and those responsible for the Panic of 1873. He had no feeling of personal responsibility because of the fiscal policies of his administration.

On March 4, 1875, Senator Andrew Johnson was in Washington, staying at the Willard Hotel. President Grant had called a special session of Congress. He said it was for the purpose of approving trade and defense treaties, but Andrew Johnson said it was for the purpose of approving the rotten administration of the southern states under radical control. Hundreds of people came to the hotel to visit Senator Johnson, and he made quite clear to all of them the course he would take in the Senate.

On the first day that he returned to the Senate, he received a standing ovation and was surrounded by friends and ancient enemies who had suddenly become almost like friends. Of the thirty-five senators who had voted to impeach him, only thirteen were still in office. He told his Senate friends that he had two purposes in returning to the Senate: to speak out against the treatment of the South and to speak out about the Grant administration.

On March 22, 1875, a resolution relative to action Grant had taken in connection with the government of Louisiana was under discussion in the Senate. Andrew Johnson chose this time to speak. He compared Grant to other men in history who had taken gifts and betrayed the people. It was a telling blow, for Grant was a great gift-taker, and if not personally corrupt in the sense that many of his appointees were, he was not strictly honorable in his approach to government. He also spoke out against the third term that Grant wanted for himself. He pleaded for justice for the South, now that a decade had passed since the crushing of the Confederacy.

"Let us come up to this work," he said, in his old fashion, "forgetting what we have been heretofore. Let us lay aside our party feelings; let us lay aside our personalities and come up to the Constitution of our country and lay it upon an altar and all stand around, resolved that the Constitution shall be preserved."

The special session ended the following day, and Andrew Johnson took the train home. At home in Greeneville, he lived a quiet life for the next few weeks. He had contracted cholera two years earlier and his health had been permanently weakened by the disease. He was sixty-eight years old and he had undergone personal trials in the past fifteen years that would weaken any man.

In July, 1865, Andrew Johnson set out by train for Carter Station, to visit his daughter Mary at her home. Eliza had gone to Mary's house a few days before. He arrived before lunch, and after that noon meal, he went to his room to rest, accompanied by his granddaughter, Lillie Stover. They talked for a few moments and then she started to the door. As she turned, she heard a thump behind her and discovered that her grandfather had fallen to the floor.

He had suffered a stroke and feared that his left side was paralyzed. The family put him into bed. He would not let them call a doctor. The next day, at almost the same time he suffered another stroke and went into a coma. Doctors were called but they could do nothing for him. Two hours after that second attack, Andrew Johnson died.

He had wanted no religious funeral services, so his body was taken back to Greeneville in a plain pine box, and there transferred to a more formal coffin. According to his wishes, his head was pillowed on the first copy of the Constitution of the United States that he had ever owned, and his body was wrapped in the flag of the United States, with its thirty-seven stars. The simple inscription: Andrew Johnson, Seventeenth President of the United States, was engraved on the silver plate that adorned the coffin. The body was placed on view in the Masonic assembly hall in Greeneville for a few hours, and then eighteen pallbearers carried the coffin to a funeral hearse and it was escorted slowly to the place that Andrew Johnson had chosen for his burial, a cone-shaped hill a half-mile from the town. A band played Webster's Funeral March, and a bugler blew taps as "the old Commoner" was buried.

Thus died the President who was a vulgar man—a common man, a man of the people. He had all the failings of the common man. He was direct. He was brutal sometimes in language and in action. He could be cruel. He could and did hate fiercely, and he acted quickly. There was no diplomacy in him. Yet he could forgive and forget, as he showed many times. He could be magnaminous in victory, as he was courageous in defeat. Above all he stood on principle, and the last fifteen years of his life were spent in vigorous support and later defense of the Constitution of the United States. He knew himself better than any other, and he chose to lay his head upon that document that he, almost alone, had defended in the years in which it was in mortal danger.

BIBLIOGRAPHY

⭐

BEARD, CHARLES AND MARY. *The Rise of American Civilization*. New York: The Macmillan Co., 1927.

BOWERS, CLAUDE G. *The Tragic Era, the Revolution After Lincoln*. Cambridge, Mass.: Houghton Mifflin Co., 1929.

BURGESS, JOHN W. *Reconstruction and the Constitution*. New York: C. Scribner's Sons, 1902.

CHADSEY, C. E. *The Struggle Between President Johnson and Congress Over Reconstruction*. New York: Columbia University, 1896.

COWAN, FRANK. *Andrew Johnson, President of the United States. Reminiscences of his Private Life and Character*. Greenesburgh, Penna.: The Oliver Publishing House, 1894.

GIPSON, LAWRENCE H. "The Statesmanship of President Johnson," *Mississippi Valley Historical Review*, Dec. 1915.

JONES, JAMES S. *The Life of Andrew Johnson*. Greeneville, Tenn.: East Tennessee Publishing Co., 1901.

SAVAGE, JOHN. *Life and Public Service of Andrew Johnson*. New York: Derby & Miller, 1866.

WINSTON, ROBERT W. *Andrew Johnson, Plebian and Patriot*. New York: H. Holt & Co., 1928.

INDEX

✩